BARRON'S BOOK NOTES

Old Testament

BARRON'S BOOK NOTES

Old Testament

BY
Geoffrey M. Horn

SERIES COORDINATOR
Murray Bromberg
Principal, Wang High School of Queens
Holliswood, New York

Past President
High School Principals Association of New York City

BARRON'S

BARRON'S EDUCATIONAL SERIES, INC.
Woodbury, New York • London • Toronto • Sydney

All inquiries should be addressed to:
Barron's Educational Series, Inc.
113 Crossways Park Drive
Woodbury, New York 11797

Library of Congress Catalog Card No. 85-4066

International Standard Book No. 0-8120-3531-3

Library of Congress Cataloging in Publication Data
Horn, Geoffrey.
  Old Testament

  (Barron's book notes)
  Bibliography: p. 189
  Summary: A guide to reading the Old Testament with
a critical and appreciative mind. Includes sample tests,
term paper suggestions, and a reading list.
  1. Bible. O.T.—Text-books. [1. Bible. O.T.—
Text-books] I. Title. II. Series.
BS1194.H63 1986   221.6′1   85-4066
ISBN 0-8120-3531-3

CONTENTS

ADVISORY BOARD

We wish to thank the following educators who helped us focus our *Book Notes* series to meet student needs and critiqued our manuscripts to provide quality materials.

The following experts reviewed the *Book Notes* manuscript on the Old Testament. The volume does not necessarily reflect their views, however.

HOW TO USE THIS BOOK

The Old Testament is a monument in the development of theology, morality, and law, the foundation stone of three of the world's great religions—Judaism, Christianity, and Islam. Moreover, it is an important documentary record, used by historians and archaeologists to understand the growth of civilization in the ancient world. But the Old Testament can also be read as a pageant of poetry and prophecy, of lyrical beauty and high drama—in other words, as one of the world's great works of literature.

You have to know how to approach literature in order to get the most out of it. This *Barron's Book Notes* volume follows a plan based on methods used by some of the best students to read a work of literature.

Begin with the guide's section on the Old Testament and its times. As you read, try to form a clear picture of the life and thought of the ancient people of Israel. The background should make it easier for you to understand the Bible's view of God, the world, and humanity's role in it.

Then go over the rest of the introductory materials—such sections as those on theology, personalities, setting, themes, style, and form of the work. Underline, or write down in your notebook, particular things to watch for, such as contrasts between peoples and personalities, key concepts of morals and law, and repeated literary devices. At this point, you may want to develop a system of symbols to use in marking your Bible text as you read. (Of course, you should only mark up a plain study Bible you own, not a fine collector's edition or a Bible that belongs to another person, to your school, or to your house of worship.) Perhaps you will want to use a different letter for each major theme of the book, a different number for each important literary device, a special color to signal important historical events. Put your marks in the margins so that you can find them again easily.

Now comes the moment you've been waiting for—the time to start reading the biblical text. You may want to put aside your *Barron's Book Notes* volume until you've completed the assigned reading. Or you may want to alternate, consulting the *Book Notes* analysis of each section as soon as you have finished reading the corresponding part of the original. Before you move on, reread crucial passages you don't understand. (Don't take this guide's analysis for granted—make up your own mind as to what the work means.)

Once you've finished the assigned sections, you may want to review them right away, so you can firm up your ideas of what the text means. You may want to leaf through the assigned readings concentrating on passages you marked with reference to major themes or historical patterns. This is also a good time to reread the *Book Notes* introductory material, which pulls together insights on specific topics.

When it comes time to prepare for a test or to write a paper, you'll already have formed ideas about the work. You'll be able to go back through it, refreshing your memory as to the exact words and events described, so that you can support your opinions with evidence drawn straight from the work. Patterns will emerge, and ideas will fall into place; your essay question or term paper will almost write itself. Give yourself a dry run with one of the sample tests in the guide. These tests present both multiple-choice and essay questions. An accompanying section gives answers to the multiple-choice questions as well as suggestions for writing the essays. If you have to select a term paper topic, you may choose one from the list of suggestions in the book. This guide also provides you with a reading list, to help you when you start research for a term paper, and a selection of stimulating or provocative passages from commentators, to spark your thinking before you write.

The Bible has been translated into English many times and in many different styles. Unless otherwise noted, all biblical quotations in this *Barron's Book Notes* volume are from the Authorized (King James) Version, the translation in which the Old Testament has made its greatest impact on English language and literature. Personal pronouns relating to God (Me, Thou, He, Him, etc.) have been consistently capitalized. You can read more about the different versions of the Old Testament in the section "Translations and Editions."

THE OLD TESTAMENT BACKGROUND

The Old Testament and Its Times

Suppose a powerful army invaded your town, destroyed your house and those of your neighbors, sacked all places of worship, and carried your entire community off to a distant land. Uprooted and unhappy, you would face the desperate task of rebuilding your life in an alien environment. Of course, your most pressing task would be to provide for immediate needs—food, clothing, shelter. But you might also begin to ask some very painful questions. Who was to blame for this terrible disaster? Why did God allow it to happen? Had you somehow failed God, or had God failed you?

Origins of the Hebrew People

This is the crisis the ancient Hebrews faced about 2500 years ago. Their entire identity as a people was based on the idea, told in the book of Genesis, that God had promised the land of Canaan to their ancestor Abraham and his children about 1500 years earlier, in other words, around the year 2000 B.C. This promise took many centuries to fulfill. The Hebrews were a migratory people, and after Abraham's death many of them settled in Egypt, to the southwest. For many years the Hebrews prospered in Egypt, but changes in Egyptian society

Brief Chronology of Old Testament Times

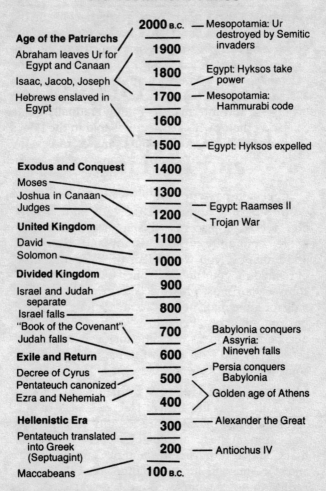

	2000 B.C.	— Mesopotamia: Ur destroyed by Semitic invaders
Age of the Patriarchs	1900	
Abraham leaves Ur for Egypt and Canaan	1800	Egypt: Hyksos take power
Isaac, Jacob, Joseph		
Hebrews enslaved in Egypt	1700	— Mesopotamia: Hammurabi code
	1600	
	1500	— Egypt: Hyksos expelled
Exodus and Conquest	1400	
Moses	1300	
Joshua in Canaan		— Egypt: Raamses II
Judges	1200	
United Kingdom		Trojan War
David	1100	
Solomon	1000	
Divided Kingdom		
Israel and Judah separate	900	
Israel falls	800	
"Book of the Covenant"	700	Babylonia conquers Assyria: Nineveh falls
Judah falls		
Exile and Return	600	
Decree of Cyrus	500	Persia conquers Babylonia
Pentateuch canonized		
Ezra and Nehemiah	400	Golden age of Athens
Hellenistic Era	300	— Alexander the Great
Pentateuch translated into Greek (Septuagint)	200	— Antiochus IV
Maccabeans	**100** B.C.	

NOTE: The traditional date for the birth of Christ is the turning point of the Western calendar, the year 1. Dates before then are labeled B.C.; dates after then are labeled A.D. The *higher* the date B.C. the *earlier* it is; the *lower* the date B.C., the closer it is to the Christian era. For years labeled A.D., the *higher* the number, the *later* the date is. Some histories of Old Testament times, especially those by Jewish scholars, replace the abbreviations B.C. and A.D. with B.C.E. and C.E., respectively.

around 1500 B.C. led to a drastic decline in the status of all non-Egyptians and—according to the book of Exodus—to the enslavement of the Hebrews. Sometime between 1300 and 1200 B.C. the Hebrews, led by Moses, fled Egypt and settled in Canaan. During the next two centuries, through conquest and intermarriage, they gradually made the land their own. (This story is told in the books of Joshua, Judges, and Samuel.) In the process, the Hebrews, who had begun as nomads with a society based on clans or tribes, developed a centralized kingship and worship based in Jerusalem.

For a few centuries the Hebrews, also called Israelites, were masters in their own land, the land of Israel. But weakened by economic rivalries, political divisions, and pagan influences, the Israelites fell prey to powerful enemy empires, first the Assyrians and then the Babylonians. In the year 586 B.C. the armies of the Babylonian king Nebuchadnezzar beseiged Jerusalem and destroyed the great Temple built by Solomon about 350 years earlier. Many hundreds of civic and religious leaders were killed, and thousands more were exiled to Babylon. This tragic story is recounted in several books of the Old Testament, notably 2 Kings, 2 Chronicles, and Jeremiah. (The "2" given before the name of the book is a shorthand way of saying "Second Book of . . . . ")

The Faith of the Hebrews

Central to the faith of the Hebrews was their belief that the land of Israel had been promised by God to their forefathers Abraham, Isaac, and Jacob. But now the Promised Land had been laid waste, and the exiled Israelites had every reason to fear that they would never see their homeland again. The

Babylonians felt certain that their victory over the Israelites proved that the gods of Babylon were more powerful than the God of the Hebrews. How were the ancient Israelites to answer this challenge and preserve their faith?

If you have ever lived away from home for any length of time, you may have felt the impulse to assimilate—to take on the language, customs, and beliefs of those around you. Surely there were many Israelites who, starting out as alien captives in Babylon, became just like their Babylonian captors. But you may also have felt the opposite impulse—the urge to hold onto your former identity, to cling to those qualities that made you special and different from those around you. Many of the exiles had this same reaction. This is why the period of exile, far from undermining the Hebrew religion, ushered in a great religious revival. The Old Testament records the words and deeds of the prophets and political leaders who made this revival possible.

The Hebrew Scriptures

No one is sure which sacred writings the Israelites brought with them to Babylon. The likelihood is, however, that the Book of Deuteronomy—the fifth book of the Old Testament—was among them. This book, a summary of the basic laws of Israel, takes the form of a long farewell address by Moses to his people before they cross the Jordan River into the Promised Land. Deuteronomy—or part of it— is probably the "Book of the Covenant" referred to in 2 Kings 23:2. (The notation "23:2" means the second verse of Chapter 23.) Many scholars believe that Deuteronomy was the first part of the Old Testament to be written down in anything like its present form. This does not mean, however, that Deuteronomy is the oldest part of the Bible. When the Israelites wrote down the Old Testament in its definitive form, they may also have included many older documents, along with a wealth of laws, legends, myths, folk tales, songs, poems, and proverbs that had been passed down orally from generation to generation.

Today, people make a clear distinction between history and legend, between myth and fact. After hearing a juicy bit of gossip about a rock group or a movie star, you might well ask, "Is that *really* true?" When you read in the Old Testament about Lot's wife turned into a pillar of salt, about Samson tearing apart a lion with his bare hands, or about the boy David slaying the giant Goliath with a slingshot, you may find yourself asking the same question. Biblical commentators have been seeking to separate fact from myth for many hundreds of years, and the biblical archaeologists now digging in the Holy Land are also trying to distinguish history from legend. Weighing all the textual and historical evidence to decide for yourself what is "really true" is a very important part of reading the Old Testament as history and as literature.

But you should bear in mind, as you read critically, that the peoples of Old Testament times did not separate fact from myth as we do. The Israelites who over the course of centuries established the text of the Old Testament thought they were weaving a seamless web. The creation of the world, the revelations to the patriarchs, the chronicles of the people of Israel, the visions of the prophets—all these, the ancient Hebrews believed, bore the unmistakable stamp of divine purpose. Today, many Christians and Jews believe the same thing,

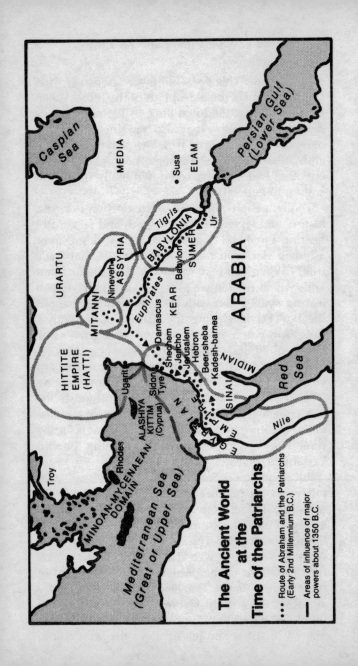

The Ancient World at the Time of the Patriarchs

•••• Route of Abraham and the Patriarchs (Early 2nd Millennium B.C.)
— Areas of influence of major powers about 1350 B.C.

although believers differ among themselves as to whether the texts are all literally true and, if not, how much interpretation they require.

Torah, Nevi'im, Ketuvim

Within the growing body of Hebrew scripture, the first five books of the Old Testament had special importance. These five books, which are familiar to us by their Greek names—Genesis, Exodus, Leviticus, Numbers, Deuteronomy—were believed to have been given by God to Moses on Mount Sinai (also called Horeb) after the Israelites had escaped from bondage in Egypt. These Five Books of Moses are often called the Pentateuch, which is Greek for "five books." In the Hebrew language, however, these books bear the name *Torah*, a word that has great significance in Judaism, the religion evolved by the Hebrews, who are today known as Jews. The root of the word *Torah* is "to teach," and the term applies not only to the teachings themselves but also to the scroll from which the Five Books of Moses are read regularly in Jewish houses of worship all over the world.

The ancient Hebrews also had special names for other sections of the Bible. The narratives by and about the ancient prophets of Israel—men such as Isaiah and Jeremiah—were called *Nevi'im*, which means "prophets" in Hebrew. (Today we usually mean by a prophet someone who can foretell the future, but the Hebrews meant something quite different—one who speaks or acts for God. Be on the lookout for this special meaning of the word "prophet" when you read about Noah, Moses, and other "spokesmen for God.") Finally, a third section of the Old Testament, consisting of proverbs, songs, psalms, and historical and pseudohistorical narratives, was called *Ketuvim*, which in Hebrew simply means "writings." Borrowing letters from Torah, Nevi'im, and Ketuvim, the Hebrews came up with the anagram *Tanak*, which they applied to the entire Old Testament. The books of the Tanak—the Hebrew Bible—constitute the whole of scripture for Jews and are the basis of the Old Testament in Roman Catholic, Protestant, and Orthodox Christian Bibles.

The Greek Influence

One term that does *not* stem from ancient Hebrew is *Bible*. The origin of this familiar English word is *byblos*, which in Greek means "book." The term *byblos* stems from the Phoenician city of Byblos (near present-day Beirut, in Lebanon), which was famous in ancient times as an exporter of papyrus.

You might be wondering at this point why so many words we use to describe the Hebrew scriptures come from Greek. The answer lies in the conquest of the land of Israel in 332 B.C. by the brilliant Macedonian Greek general Alexander the Great. The impact of Greek power and culture on the Hebrews was so overwhelming that Greek became a common language in Israel, and knowledge of Hebrew was confined to only a few scholars. To prevent knowledge of the Hebrew scriptures from dying out along with the use of Hebrew, scholars during the third century B.C.—the century after Alexander conquered the Holy Land—translated the books of the Bible into Greek. This translation became known as the Septuagint ("seventy") in honor of the 70 (or 72) translators who composed it.

The Old Testament and the New

Old Testament, a term commonly used in English but frowned upon in Jewish scholarship, has its origins in the birth and growth of Christianity during Roman times. Today it is common to think of Judaism and Christianity as completely separate religions, with different beliefs, holidays, and places of worship. But the fact is that Christianity developed out of Judaism. Jesus of Nazareth was a Jew, and most of his early followers were Jewish. They had been raised to believe in the Jewish God (as opposed to the pagan gods of the Greeks and Romans) and to revere the Jewish scriptures. The disciples of Jesus did not think they were starting a new religion. Rather, they believed that the coming of Jesus as the Messiah (or, in Greek, *Christos*, or Christ) was the fulfillment of prophecies contained in the Jewish scriptures.

The split between Christianity and Judaism developed between A.D. 50 and A.D. 150, as the Jewish authorities rejected the claims made for Jesus and as the followers of Christ sought to spread their beliefs and define the differences between the Christian and Jewish faiths. In the process, these early Christians developed their own body of writings, consisting of narratives of the life of Jesus and documents explaining their beliefs to fellow Christians, pagans, and Jews. The early Christians accepted the Jewish belief that God had made a special agreement, or covenant, with Abraham. (You should keep this idea of a covenant in mind as you read the Book of Genesis.) But the Christians also believed that the birth and crucifixion of Jesus marked a turning point in Jewish history. Because the Jews did not recognize Jesus as the Messiah, early Christians concluded that the Jews had forfeited their special relationship with God. Christians came to believe that those who showed faith in Jesus had inherited the covenant and, with it, God's special favor.

The word *testament* comes from a Greek root meaning "to bear witness"; in church Latin, *testamentum* means "covenant." By calling the ancient Jewish scriptures the *Old* Testament and the basic writings of Christianity the *New* Testament, the Christians were really saying that the new covenant—belief in Jesus as Savior and Christ—had replaced the old. Many Jewish writers, rejecting this Christian version of Jewish history, use the terms *Hebrew Bible* and *Tanak* (also spelled *Tanakh* and *Tanach*) rather than *Old Testament*.

Enduring Power of the Old Testament

Why should the Old Testament, portraying the experiences and beliefs of the ancient Hebrews, have retained its importance over so many centuries and among so many different peoples? One answer, maintained by many traditionalists, is that the Old Testament is the unchanging word of God. The Old Testament is thus the infallible record of God's revelations to and through the Hebrew people. This is the view of orthodox Jews and fundamentalist Christians. After reading the Old Testament, you too may share their belief, but that decision is yours alone to make. Nor is it necessary to believe that every word in the Old Testament is literally true in order to appreciate the power and beauty of its vision. Those who depart from literalist views maintain that even if the Old Testament is the word of God, it was written with the hand of man. How, they ask, can we expect it to be wholly free of human imperfection?

You might want to consider another way of looking at the uniquely enduring power of the Old Testament. At various times in history, Christians have come into conflict with Jews, Protestants have fought against Roman Catholics, and Muslims have warred with all three. But all these different and sometimes bitterly antagonistic peoples have looked to the Old Testament for aspects of their most basic identity. For the Jews, the Old Testament is a living record of peoplehood. Even in their periods of most profound suffering and widest dispersion, the Jews could look to the Tanak as a chronicle of their continuity as a people over a period of 1600 years, from the time of Abraham to the return from Babylonian exile. The early Christians looked to the prophecies of the Old Testament to establish their claim that God had foretold the coming of Jesus and chosen the Jews to receive this great new revelation. The Protestants of the Reformation period turned to the Old Testament to support their argument that the Roman Catholic Church had strayed from the word of God, and that the Protestants were themselves the true bearers of God's covenant. The Muslims also would find in the Old Testament a major source of their beliefs and identity. They honored the Hebrew Bible for its revelation to the world that God was one, and saw in the figure of Abraham's son Ishmael the founder of their race.

The Development of the Canon

The next time you're in a library or bookstore, take a few moments to browse in the religious books section. If the library or bookstore is a good one, you'll see many different translations and editions of the Bible, along with the sacred books of other religions—Buddhism, Taoism, Hinduism, Islam. The surprising thing is that, like the Old and New Testaments, a great many of these texts were first written down or compiled during the 1200-year period between 500 B.C. and A.D. 700. Moreover, all these sacred books are anthologies. Some of these texts derive their unity from the presence of a central human figure—Buddha in the Buddhist *sutras*, Jesus in the New Testament, Muhammad in the Koran—but even these works of scripture are collections. The earliest Buddhist scriptures were not written down until centuries after the time of Buddha; the New Testament consists of writings *about* Jesus, not by him; and even though Muhammad is said to have dictated to his secretaries his revelations from God, or Allah, the definitive version of the Koran did not appear until about two decades after his death.

There are special problems in understanding how and when this anthology called the Old Testament came to be written. For centuries, the ancient Hebrews had no written language. The oldest known Hebrew inscription dates from the ninth century B.C., but the events described in the Torah extend back to 2000 B.C. and even earlier. Moreover, although commentaries indicate that the order of the Hebrew Bible was well established by the time of Jesus, the oldest known manuscript of the complete Hebrew text dates from the tenth century A.D., almost a thousand years later. Scholars have learned much about individual books of the Old Testament from the hundreds of separate manuscripts and manuscript fragments in Greek, Hebrew, and Aramaic. But even the richest source of such evidence, the Dead Sea Scrolls, which were inscribed between 200 B.C. and A.D. 100, offers Hebrew and Aramaic versions of texts that must first have been written down centuries earlier.

Sources of the Pentateuch

When you write a research paper, you list your sources at the end. Anyone who examines your bibliography will immediately know the books, articles, and other documents you consulted before you wrote your piece.

But the Old Testament has no bibliography. No investigative reporter interviewed the authors to find out what sources they used. Although the Hebrew Bible makes mention of the "Book of the Covenant" and of Ezra's reading the "Book of the Law of Moses" to the Israelites in assembly (Nehemiah 8:1–8), no such ancient books have survived independently—that is, outside the Old Testament itself.

For the orthodox Jew and the fundamentalist Christian, this lack of authenticated documentary sources does not present a problem. Their answer is that the sole source of the Bible is divine inspiration. The Bible comes from God. Any speculation about other sources is irrelevant.

For modern scholars, however, the problem is acute. Archaeologists, historians, and students of comparative religion need to know why and how Judaism developed as it did. Obviously, they cannot go to a public library and "check" the sources of the Old Testament as your teacher or professor can check the sources of your research paper. What they can do, however, is to compare the Old Testament text with what they know of neighboring cultures in order to draw parallels and make connections between what the Bible says and what other cultures believed.

You can better understand the story of Noah (Genesis 7–8) if you know the flood stories written down by other Middle Eastern peoples. You can enrich your understanding of the covenant between God and the Hebrew patriarchs by learning about the kinds of legal contracts that other peoples used. And you can more fully appreciate the law code of the Pentateuch if you compare it to the great Code of Hammurabi, inscribed in Babylonia about 500 years before the time of Moses.

The Critical Approach

During the nineteenth century, a group of German scholars, focusing on what they saw as discrepancies of style and content within the Five Books of Moses, launched an attack on the belief that all the books of the Pentateuch had been given to Moses at the same time and exactly as we have them. Instead, these biblical critics argued—and most moden scholars now agree—that different parts of the Pentateuch were written down by different people at different times. (Which parts were written at which times, and exactly how these different narratives were woven together, remain subjects of dispute.)

The German critics identified several different "authors" of the Pentateuch and distinguished them by the names they applied to God. According to the critics' view, most of Genesis was written by "J," so-called because of that author's persistent use of YHWH, or Yahweh (the Y is given as a J in German). A second writer, responsible for part of Genesis and most of Exodus and Numbers, was called "E" because of repeated references to God as Elohim. (For more on the Old Testament names for God, see the section "God in the Old Testament.") Other important writers identified by the German critics were "D," the author of Deuteronomy, and "P," who was credited with authorship of the first chapter of Genesis, the Book of Leviticus, and other priestly documents. These authors were thought to have lived between the ninth and the fifth centuries B.C.

The German critics' argument that the Pentateuch was written by different writers at different times is sometimes called the "documentary hypothesis," but it is important to remember that no such clearly identifiable "documents" have survived. The J writer and the P writer, if they existed, left no other samples of their work and no clear statement—outside the Bible itself—of their beliefs and intentions.

Critical theory offers modern scholars a powerful tool for analyzing the Old Testament and tracing its chronological development. However, critical theory has been unable to dislodge the belief that the ultimate source of the Pentateuch was Moses or God, which is exactly what orthodox opinion, rejecting both the methods and conclusions of the biblical critics, continues to maintain. Even on its own terms, all that the "documentary hypothesis" has thus far been able to establish conclusively is that (1) for a long time the biblical traditions of the Hebrews were passed down either orally or in scrolls that have since been lost and (2) the language and outlook of the Hebrews changed over the very long period during which the different parts of the Pentateuch were edited and written down.

Formation of the Canon

Why are some books included in the Old Testament and not others? Who decided that the canon of the Old Testament—the number, order, and contents of the accepted books—had to be closed, and when was that decision made? If variant versions of a sacred text existed, how did the editors of the Old Testament choose which version to include?

Such questions become inescapable when we consider the fact that although Catholic, Protestant, and Jewish editions of the Bible agree on thirty-nine books of the Old Testament, the Catholic version includes several books and parts of books that Jewish and Protestant editions omit. Moreover, many other documents have at various times been considered for inclusion in the Old Testament. Some of these, now excluded from virtually all editions, are called *Pseudepigrapha* (literally, "falsely inscribed"); others, excluded by Jewish editions, considered canonical in Catholic editions, and consigned to a special edition in some Protestant editions, are called *Apocrypha* (literally, "unknown, spurious").

The distinction between Apocrypha and Pseudepigrapha is complicated, but you will not go far wrong if you look at the circle diagram on the following page. At the core of the Old Testament is the Pentateuch, thought by traditionalists to have come directly from God. In the ring surrounding the Pentateuch are the prophetic, historical, and wisdom books, which Judaism, Roman Catholicism, and Protestantism all treat as divinely inspired. The Apocrypha in the next ring consists of books regarded by the Protestant reformer Martin Luther as being worthy of study but lacking the force of holy writ. (Also included in the Apocrypha are certain sections of the books of Esther and Daniel that are not considered canonical by Protestants and Jews. All three religious traditions consider the books themselves as part of the canon, however.) From a Roman Catholic point of view the books of the Apocrypha *are* holy writ, and from a Jewish standpoint these books are no different from the Pseudepigrapha, which all faiths agree have no place in the biblical canon. (The Pseudepigrapha are sometimes called noncanonical or extracanonical works.)

Most of the Apocrypha and Pseudepigrapha fall into the categories of historical works or wisdom

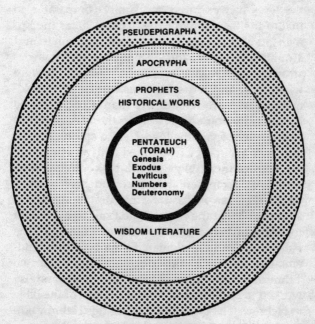

The Old Testament:
Canonical and Extracanonical Works

literature, which in the Hebrew Bible make up the Ketuvim. By the time of the Septuagint (the first translation of the Hebrew Bible into Greek), the canon of the Pentateuch and the prophets had been reasonably well established. The editors of the Septuagint must also have had some basis on which to select the Ketuvim, but we do not know what their criteria were. One thing we do know is that some books included were relatively late: 1 and 2 Maccabees, for example, deal with events in the second century B.C.

Jewish and Christian Bibles

By the time the New Testament was taking shape, the Jews had endured a calamity comparable to that of the Babylonian Exile. In A.D. 70, as the Romans moved to suppress a Jewish rebellion in and around Jerusalem, the Second Temple was destroyed, most Jewish communal institutions were wiped out, and Jerusalem was sacked by the Romans even more relentlessly than it had been by Nebuchadnezzar's troops more than six centuries earlier. Once again the Jews faced a spiritual crisis, and once again they responded with an attempt to reconstruct their religious life by codifying their scriptures. Commentaries that had been written on the Bible, as well as new interpretations by and anecdotes about the sages of Judaism, were brought together in two huge anthologies known as the Palestinian and Babylonian Talmuds. In the academies of Palestine and Babylonia where the two Talmuds were compiled, rabbinical scholars also worked to establish a definitive version of the Bible in Hebrew. The task of perfecting this Hebrew edition, which is known as the *Masorah* ("transmission"), or the Masoretic text, went on from Roman times into the Middle Ages. Today, Jewish editions of the Hebrew Bible still follow the order of the Masoretic text. Medieval Christian editions of the Old Testament, on the other hand, were based on the Greek version, or Septuagint, as translated into church Latin. The Roman Catholic version of the Old Testament follows this medieval tradition, but many Protestant editions reflect a revival of Hebrew scholarship at the beginning of the Renaissance.

The criteria used to establish the Jewish canon after the destruction of the Second Temple are relatively clear. First, no book could be more recent than the time of Ezra—the fifth century B.C.—when, according to popular belief, divine inspiration had ceased. Second, the language had to be Hebrew, not Aramaic or Greek. Third, the text had to have some history of use within the Jewish community. Fourth, the teachings had to be in the mainstream of Jewish religious thought as defined by the Pharisees, the dominant Jewish sect after Rome crushed Jerusalem. Application of the first criterion meant that some books included in the Septuagint were now excluded from the Hebrew Bible. Of course, exceptions were made, generally when a text failed one of the tests but met the others. For example, portions of Ezra, Jeremiah, and Daniel are in Aramaic.

The missionaries who carried the message of Christianity throughout the Mediterranean world frequently referred to the Jewish scriptures. But these missionaries were often Greek-speakers, preaching to Greek-speaking audiences, and the scriptures they quoted were in Greek. Thus, even as the rabbis of talmudic times were narrowing down the Hebrew canon, the early Christians in-

corporated into their teachings the full range of
Septuagint texts. The Septuagint formally entered
the canon of Catholic scripture at the church coun-
cil, or synod, of Hippo in A.D. 393. In subsequent
centuries the authority of the Apocrypha—those
books the Septuagint included but the Masoretic
text didn't—rose or fell depending upon the status
of Hebrew scholarship: the more prestige attached
to the Hebrew texts, the more the books of the
Apocrypha were called into question. The Protestant downgrading of the Apocrypha was based, in
part, on the fact that the Catholic Church cited
such Septuagint texts as authority for the idea of
purgatory and certain other doctrines the Protestants denied.

THE OLD TESTAMENT CANON

Jewish	Protestant	Roman Catholic
LAW (TORAH)	PENTATEUCH	PENTATEUCH
Genesis	Genesis	Genesis
Exodus	Exodus	Exodus
Leviticus	Leviticus	Leviticus
Numbers	Numbers	Numbers
Deuteronomy	Deuteronomy	Deuteronomy
PROPHETS (NEVI'IM)	HISTORICAL BOOKS	HISTORICAL BOOKS
Joshua	Joshua	Joshua
Judges	Judges	Judges
1 Samuel	Ruth	Ruth
2 Samuel	1 Samuel	1 Samuel
1 Kings	2 Samuel	2 Samuel
2 Kings	1 Kings	1 Kings
Isaiah	2 Kings	2 Kings
Jeremiah	1 Chronicles	1 Chronicles

THE OLD TESTAMENT CANON (cont.)

Jewish	*Protestant*	*Roman Catholic*
Ezekiel	2 Chronicles	2 Chronicles
The Twelve	Ezra	Ezra
Hosea	Nehemiah	Nehemiah
Joel	Esther	*Tobit
Amos		*Judith
Obadiah		Esther
Jonah		*1 Maccabees
Micah		*2 Maccabees
Nahum	**POETIC**	**WISDOM LIT-**
Habakkuk	**BOOKS**	**ERATURE**
Zephaniah	Job	Job
Haggai	Psalms	Psalms
Zechariah	Proverbs	Proverbs
Malachi	Ecclesiastes	Ecclesiastes
	Song of	Song of Songs
WRITINGS	Solomon	*Wisdom
(KETUVIM)		*Sirach
Psalms		
Proverbs	**PROPHETIC**	**PROPHETIC**
Job	**BOOKS**	**BOOKS**
Song of Songs	Isaiah	Isaiah
Ruth	Jeremiah	Jeremiah
Lamentations	Lamentations	Lamentations
Ecclesiastes	Ezekiel	*Baruch
Esther	Daniel	Ezekiel

*Books marked with an asterisk appear in the Septuagint and the medieval Latin editions of the Bible but not in the Masoretic text. They have been accepted into the canon of the Roman Catholic Bible but not of the Protestant and Jewish versions. These books, as well as other writings, appear in some Protestant Bibles as appendices. The technical term for these additional works is Apocrypha, a Greek word that literally means "hidden" or "unknown." In this *Barron's Guide*, these books are considered as a group under the heading "Apocrypha and Pseudepigrapha" at the end of the section Books of the Old Testament.

THE OLD TESTAMENT CANON (cont.)

Jewish	Protestant	Roman Catholic
Daniel	Hosea	Daniel
Ezra	Joel	Hosea
Nehemiah	Amos	Joel
1 Chronicles	Obadiah	Amos
2 Chronicles	Jonah	Obadiah
	Micah	Jonah
	Nahum	Micah
	Habakkuk	Nahum
	Zephaniah	Habakkuk
	Haggai	Zephaniah
	Zechariah	Haggai
	Malachi	Zechariah
		Malachi

God in the Old Testament

Do you believe in God? If you answered yes to that question, do you also believe that God, in your own time, perhaps on this very day, could speak to you from a burning bush, bet with Satan to test your faith, free an entire people from slavery, make the seas divide, or destroy the world by flood or fire? If someone you knew told you that God had spoken directly to him, and that he was now speaking as God's prophet, would you believe him, or would you tell him he was crazy? If you were a father and God told you to prepare to kill your favorite young son as a sacrifice to Him, would you do it?

If you are beginning to feel a little confused or doubtful, don't be embarrassed. As you grow and develop, even as you read the Old Testament, your ideas about God may very well change. This is understandable, because a close reading of the Old Testament shows that the ancient Hebrews' own ideas about God changed over the centuries.

Names of God

Of course, you know the Bible was not originally written in English, so the ancient Hebrews never wrote or heard the word "God." In the Old Testament, God has several different names. The ones that appear most frequently are

- *El Elyon*, meaning "the Most High";
- *El Shaddai*, usually rendered in English as "God Almighty";
- *Elohim*, a noun applied in the plural form to the pagan gods (or any supernatural beings) and in the singular to the God of Israel;
- *Adonai*, meaning "the Lord"; and
- *Yahweh* (also *Jahweh* or *Jehovah*), the personal name of the God of Israel, a name so holy that its four Hebrew consonants (equivalent to YHWH), known as the Tetragrammaton, have long been the object of mystic contemplation.

Experienced translators of and commentators on the original Hebrew text have long used the different names of God as clues to interpretation. For example, the rabbis whose views are recorded in the Talmud (second to fifth centuries A.D.) believed that the use of the name YHWH was meant to emphasize God's mercy, while the name Elohim reflected God's role as judge. At Genesis 15:2 and 15:8, Abraham refers to God as Adonai; scholars have used the knowledge that *adon* in the Bible also means someone having legal authority (as we might say the "lord of the manor") to explain the covenant God made with Abraham.

Monotheism vs. Polytheism

In order to appreciate the revolutionary quality of Hebrew monotheism, or belief in one God, you have to know how other ancient peoples thought of the powers that ruled the universe. Except for the Hebrews, virtually all peoples of the ancient Near East during the biblical period were poly-theistic; that is, they believed in many gods. It is no exaggeration to say that the ancient Mesopo-tamians recognized thousands of gods. Each city had a god. Each town had a god. Each village or tribe had a god. Each household had its own wooden or clay idols, which supposedly took on godlike powers if the right words were uttered and the correct sacrifices performed. Each aspect of na-ture had its own god or goddess; if enough rain did not fall, if the sun did not shine, if crops did not grow, if a woman did not bear children, this occurred because the gods of rain or sun or fertility were angry or, worse still, at war with each other. The kind of fear and frustration that belief in many gods could lead to is well expressed in this ancient Mesopotamian lament:

> The god whom I know or do not know has
>   oppressed me;
> The goddess whom I know or do not know has
>   placed suffering upon me.
> Although I am constantly looking for help, no
>   one takes me by the hand;
> When I weep they do not come to my side.

God as a Hero

No such doubt afflicts the author of Genesis 1:1, the first line of the Old Testament: "In the begin-ning God created the heaven and the earth." It has been said that God is the hero of the Old Testa-ment, and in Genesis you will meet God in all His incomparable and solitary grandeur. No "proof" of the existence of God is offered, nor does Genesis bother to explain *why* God created the universe. Rather, the fact of creation is a given, the ultimate tribute to God's awesome powers. Nor does Genesis offer the slightest hint that in creating the universe, God worked indirectly, through the forces of nature (some writers have used this line of argument in attempting to reconcile the biblical account of creation with modern scientific discoveries in biology and astronomy). Creation is direct, through God's own word and spirit. Indeed, directness is the key to God's actions throughout the Pentateuch. God speaks directly to Adam and Eve, to Noah, to Abraham, and to Moses. The Ten Commandments (Exodus 20) are dictated directly by God to Moses and then delivered by Moses to the people of Israel.

Changing Concepts of God
In the later books of the Old Testament, however, you should see a different pattern beginning to emerge. Only rarely in these later books does God intervene directly in human affairs. God's presence is still felt in the Law of Moses, in the covenant with Abraham, in the divine mission of the people of Israel, in the inspiration of the prophets. But when the people of Israel turn away from God, their punishment comes not directly from the Lord but through the agency of warlike nations. When the people of Israel turn back to holiness, their reward is not some new miracle but brave leaders and a prosperous economy.

In these later writings, God appears not so much as an agent in history as an interpretation of history. You can see this difference between these two ways of thinking about God and history if you imagine a terrible automobile accident at an intersection where the traffic light is not working. In trying to find some reason for the car crash, you might, if you consider God to be an agent in the accident, say, "The hand of God must have reached down from heaven and switched off the light." Alternatively, you might treat God as an explanation for or interpretation of the accident by shaking your head sadly and saying, "It all must be part of God's plan." (Of course, you might not mention God at all, but might instead complain loudly to city authorities about poor maintenance of traffic control equipment!)

Many modern writers on the Old Testament and Israelite history believe that the ancient Hebrews' ideas about God changed in another important way. The appearance of God before Abraham and His agreement to protect the patriarch's descendants as long as they would follow His laws is consistent with the view of the God of Israel as a tribal god— in other words, as one god among many. Exodus 15:11 ("Who is like unto Thee, O Lord, among the gods?") and Exodus 20:3 ("Thou shalt have no other gods before Me") can both be read as statements that other gods did exist, though none was so powerful as Yahweh. However, other parts of the Bible show a much broader conception. This can be seen in the opening of Genesis, where God appears not just as the defender of a particular clan or people but as the creator of the entire universe. Notice as you read the words of the prophets how the God of Israel is shown to be the God of all peoples, even those that do not know or accept Him.

Of course, you will have many occasions to consider the nature and powers of God as you read the Old Testament and the notes in this guide on each book of the Hebrew Bible. But there is one thing you should be aware of from the beginning. Although the Bible uses male words in referring to God—King, Father, He, His, Him—religious writers have long been troubled by the idea that to consider God as a male is to make him too manlike (or humanlike) and therefore to limit or diminish His powers. The use of exclusively male language also is a stumbling block for women who reject a society and theology based on patriarchy and female subordination. Several recent translations for purposes of worship have experimented with substituting "Sovereign" for "Lord," "Ruler" for "King," and "Parent" for "Father." This whole question is very controversial and will surely remain so for a long time to come.

Personalities

If God is *the* hero of the Old Testament, what about the hundreds of other men and women who give the Hebrew Bible its epic scope? One way to recognize how influential these biblical personalities are is to recall how many Adams, Davids, Ruths, Rebeccas, and Rachels you have known and grown up with. Such names have remained popular over the centuries at least in part because their biblical namesakes were regarded as heroes and heroines, as worthy models of behavior.

Heroism Without Hero Worship

Perhaps you have heard of something called hero worship. You are a hero worshiper if you are so excited by a person's strengths that you cannot see his or her weaknesses. Today the objects of hero worship are usually popular music, film, and sports stars, but in ancient times they tended to be kings, conquerors, and tribal leaders. It was common among ancient peoples to regard the ruler as a kind of god, and many hymns were composed to honor the Mesopotamian kings and Egyptian pharaohs.

The writers of the Old Testament were very much aware of the dangers of hero worship. Since the religion of the Hebrews was based on monotheism, or belief in one God, there could be only one fit object of worship: God Himself. Viewed in this light, the tendency to worship earthly kings, even worthy ancestors, left the way open to polytheism and idolatry. Thus, in the Old Testament, only God is faultless. Every human personality—even the greatest of the Israelites—is shown to have human failings. Moreover, the greater the leader, the stricter the standards applied.

Strengths and Weaknesses

Consider a few examples you will encounter in your reading. Adam and Eve, regarded by the Bible as our first parents, are created by God in His own image, but their disobedience leads to their expulsion from the Garden of Eden and to a curse on all humankind. Notice how Noah is called "a just man and perfect in his generations" (Genesis 6:9) when God chooses him to build the ark that will protect a remnant of God's creation from the coming flood. Later, however, when the flood waters have subsided, Noah will become a wine maker, and his sons will find him lying naked and drunk. The magnificent Moses, chosen by God to bring freedom and law to the children of Israel, is not permitted to enter the Promised Land because he disobeys a divine command in one of his typical displays of anger (Numbers 20:7–13).

You will not find any biblical character more remarkable than David, the shepherd, poet, warrior, rebel, and king. For many centuries in Western Europe, writers on politics cited David and his son Solomon as the supreme models of good government. But if you read carefully, you will see that neither man is free from blemish. The prophet Nathan bitterly denounces King David for lusting after the beautiful Bathsheba and arranging to have her husband murdered (2 Samuel 12:1–15). As for Solomon, although the Hebrew Bible praises him as a wise king and judge, it also makes clear that his use of forced labor in building spendid royal cities paved the way for the period of divisiveness and rebellion that followed his death.

As you read about each of these biblical personalities, you should attempt to weigh the hero's weaknesses and strengths to arrive at a balanced judgment. Generally, the Old Testament presents each character as worthy to the extent that he follows the ways of God, and as flawed to the extent that he substitutes his own desires for the divine will. In assessing how each biblical figure achieves heroic stature or goes astray, you should also ask yourself what each episode reveals about the nature of the Old Testament God and the kind of obedience He demands.

Other Elements
SETTING

Imagine the money a clever tour promoter could make with a well-publicized trip through Old Testament lands.The pilgrims would start with a picnic lunch in the Garden of Eden; spend the night on Mount Ararat, where Noah's ark came to rest; cross the Red Sea at the precise point where the Israelites crossed it; and ascend Mount Sinai, following in the footsteps of Moses. If you think you'd like to take or organize such a tour, better think again: after years of intensive research, scholars have not been able to establish the exact location of any of these places.

Problems in Biblical History

Eden, which means "delight" in Hebrew, probably stems from the Sumerian word *Edinn*, a general name for the fertile plain of Babylon. There is a mountain called Ararat in eastern Turkey, but no reputable scholar has been able to prove that Noah's ark stopped there; more likely, the Old Testament means the Armenian mountains that belonged to an empire the ancients knew as Urartu. As for the Red Sea, which separates Egypt from the Arabian Peninsula, most experts now say the correct translation of the Hebrew *yam suf* is "Sea of Reeds," location unknown. Nor has the exact route of the Exodus been established. Although, by tradition, a peak in the Sinai Peninsula called Jabal Musa (Arabic for "Mountain of Moses") is thought to be the site where Moses received the Ten Commandments, there is no proof, and modern opinion remains divided. An interesting mixed case is the town of Jericho, one of the world's most ancient fortified cities. At Jericho, archaeologists have found mud-brick dwellings and public buildings that are nearly 9000 years old; but no trace of the walls supposedly destroyed by Joshua around 1200 B.C. has ever been discovered.

Archaeological Findings

If you want to argue that much of the Old Testament is merely legend, not fact, all this evidence is grist for your mill. But you should also be aware of the many biblical sites that archaeologists have confirmed since the nineteenth century. The settlement called "Ur of the Chaldees" in Genesis 11 has been identified as an ancient Mesopotamian city near the right bank of the Euphrates River; it is known that Ur fell to nomadic invaders around 2000 B.C., about the same time that, according to the biblical narrative, Abraham and his family set out for the Promised Land. Remains of an Israelite fortress have been found at Kadesh-barnea, an oasis in the northern Sinai Desert that the Bible mentions as a gathering place for the Hebrews after they left Egypt. Some of the most important finds have been made at Hazor and Megiddo, two cities in northern Israel that were built by King Solomon during the tenth century B.C. And, of course, there is no doubt about the location of Jerusalem, which King David chose as his royal capital. This city, holy to Jews, Christians, and Muslims alike, has long been studied by archaeologists, and today Jerusalem is once again the capital of a Jewish state.

The World of the Old Testament

The Old Testament contains many dozens of place-names, and it would be foolish to try to memorize them all. But as you read, you should try to fix in your mind a rough geography of the biblical world. At the center of the biblical world, physically as well as spiritually, is the land of Israel. Israel's political boundaries have shifted over the centuries, but you won't go far wrong if you think of the land as bounded by the Great or Upper Sea (now the Mediterranean Sea) to the west, the Jordan River to the east, Lebanon to the north, and the Sinai Desert and Red Sea to the south. As you may have noticed already, this land has many names: Canaan, the Promised Land, Israel, Judah and Israel (in the time of the divided kingdom), Judea and Samaria, Palestine (from Roman times until the establishment of the State of Israel in 1948), and the Holy Land.

Why is so much of the Old Testament taken up with war and conquest? One reason is that Israel was at the very center of the economy of the Middle East. Copper was mined in the Sinai, and wheat, barley, dates, and fruit trees flourished. The ancient Hebrews were a pastoral people, and if you recall that David was originally a shepherd, you will not be surprised to hear that sheep-raising also played a major role in the economy. Passing through the land of Israel was a route now known by the Latin name *Via Maris* ("way of the sea"), the main trade route linking Egypt in the southwest with Assyria in the northeast and with the Fertile Crescent of Mesopotamia in the east, extending along the Tigris and Euphrates rivers to the Lower Sea (now the Persian or Arabian Gulf). This means that Israel was buffeted by cultural influences from each of these great civilizations, even as it fell prey to each empire's program of military and economic expansion. Because the Via Maris was a route for people as well as commerce, Israel was also a target of migrating tribes who had left their own lands because of exhaustion of grazing lands, natural disaster, or military defeat. All these economic, political, and cultural factors combined to enhance the importance of what was otherwise a rather small and insignificant land.

Peoples of the Old Testament

The Old Testament records many warnings to the Hebrews not to intermarry with neighboring peoples, in order to avoid polluting the worship of Yahweh with alien cult practices. The fact is, however, that the ancient Hebrews not only intermarried with but also learned from their neighbors, and the history of the ancient Hebrews cannot be understood apart from the history of other Near Eastern peoples.

Interaction with the **Egyptians** began as early as the time of Abraham and was most intense during the centuries between Joseph and Moses. This rich civilization, which developed more than 5000 years ago, was based on cultivation of the Nile Delta. The enduring monuments of that civilization are the pyramids, built by the Egyptian kings (pharaohs)—who were believed to descend from the sun-god Ra—as their own huge tombs. Traditionally, Egyptian religion was polytheistic. However, one pharaoh, Akhnaten, did try to stamp out polytheism and impose on Egypt the uniform worship of a single solar deity. One fascinating aspect of this period for students of the Old Testament is that Akhnaten reigned during the fourteenth century B.C., at a time when the children of Israel may already have become slaves.

Contact with the peoples of Mesopotamia likewise began as early as Abraham. Notable among the many peoples who inhabited the Fertile Crescent were the **Sumerians**, whose empire collapsed around 2000 B.C., and the **Babylonians**, whose first and greatest ruler (during the eighteenth century B.C.) was Hammurabi. The **Chaldeans** dominated the Mesopotamian region from the ninth to the sixth centuries B.C., warring with the **Assyrians** to the northwest. From the Chaldean dynasty arose the new Babylonian empire, under Nebuchadnezzar, that ravaged Jerusalem and forced the Hebrews into exile. Having conquered Assyria and Judah, the new Babylonian rulers were themselves conquered in the sixth century B.C. by the **Persians**. The Persian era, which lasted for a little more than 200 years, was brought to an abrupt halt by Alexander the Great, who spread the civilization of the **Greeks** throughout the Near East.

Other biblical peoples you should know include the **Philistines**, "Sea Peoples" who settled the coastal region as the Hebrews were penetrating the interior of Canaan, and who were among the Israelites' fiercest rivals; the Philistines figure prominently in the stories of Samson, Saul, and David. The **Phoenicians** (called Sidonians in the Old Testament), who lived to the north, along the coast of what is now Lebanon, were renowned as sea traders; their impact on the culture of the Near East included development of the alphabet, the invention of glass, the making of dyes (including the prized Tyrian purple) and the worship of Baal and Astarte. Related to the Phoenicians were the **Canaanites** (worshipers of Baal and Ashtoreth), whom the Israelites conquered and absorbed. From the **Arameans**, who first settled in the area now known as Syria, came the Aramaic language, in which some passages of the Old Testament are written.

MAJOR THEMES

The Old Testament is an epic work, from which many morals and historical lessons may be drawn. This chapter can't possibly list them all. As you read the Old Testament, you should be sensitive to the many persistent major themes:

- Relations between men and women (Adam and Eve, Samson and Delilah, Ruth and Boaz, David and Bathsheba, Esther and Ahasuerus)
- Relations between parents and children (Abraham and Isaac, Isaac and Jacob, Jacob and Joseph, David and Absalom)
- Relations between siblings (Cain and Abel, Esau and Jacob, Joseph and his brothers, Moses and Aaron)
- The favored destiny of a younger or youngest child (Isaac, Jacob, Joseph, David)
- The significance of name changes as indications of a change in personality and destiny (Abram-Abraham, Sarai-Sarah, Jacob-Israel, Oshea-Joshua)
- God as a miracle worker (Sarah's pregnancy, the Exodus story, Joshua at Jericho, Elijah)
- The bond between the people of Israel and the land of Israel (covenant of Abraham, settlement of Canaan, Babylonian Exile, decree of Cyrus)
- The burdens of the prophet (Moses, Jeremiah, Jonah)

These themes are all essential to an understanding of the Old Testament as a work of literature; you should try to remember them when reading the assigned passages, reviewing for an exam, or choosing a term paper topic. But it is also important to keep in mind a few basic ideas that underlie the Old Testament as a work of religious thought.

1. THE OLD TESTAMENT TELLS THE STORY OF THE HEBREW PEOPLE.

Central to the Hebrew Bible is the story of how the ancient Hebrews come to see themselves as a chosen people, become slaves and then escape from

Egypt, receive their code of law through Moses, establish themselves in the Promised Land, and defend themselves against their enemies. Coupled with this outer political history of the Hebrews is an inner spiritual history, embracing the idea of a covenant with God, a growing belief in the ideals of peace and social justice and in the coming of a Messiah, and a persistent conflict between those few who speak for God—the prophets—and the masses of people whose faith wavers and falters.

2. GOD HAS A SPECIAL RELATIONSHIP WITH THE HEBREW PEOPLE.

The book of Genesis makes clear the Hebrew belief that the very same all-powerful and all-knowing God who created the universe revealed Himself to the Hebrew patriarchs. To the Hebrew people Yahweh makes these gifts: the Promised Land and the covenant relationship, as expressed through Divine Law, or Torah. From the Hebrew people Yahweh expects one thing: absolute obedience. (Keep this requirement in mind as you read about Abraham and Isaac at Genesis 22.) God also reigns over other peoples and expects their actions to be righteous and just, but the special blessings given to the Hebrews impose on them special obligations (notably male circumcision) from which other peoples are exempt.

3. GOD IN THE OLD TESTAMENT IS A LAWGIVER WHO PUNISHES DISOBEDIENCE BUT REWARDS OBEDIENCE AND REPENTANCE.

The theme of disobedience and punishment appears from the outset, in the story of Adam and Eve. Much of the Pentateuch consists of a long list of commandments conveyed through Moses to the

Hebrew people. The belief that God will greet repentance with mercy runs throughout the prophetic books (look, for example, at the Book of Hosea).

4. GOD VALUES RIGHT ACTION MORE THAN EMPTY RITUAL.

Many laws in the Pentateuch deal with work, rest, sex, hygiene, and social responsibilities. These, basically, are the obligations of righteousness and respect you owe to yourself and to your family, friends, and other people. But many other laws in the Torah concern specific religious obligations to God. Among the Hebrews, these laws were the responsibility of a priestly caste, which maintained the Temple in Jerusalem and supervised the animal sacrifices made there. A powerful theme in the prophetic books is that ritual without righteousness is an insult to God (see, for example, Isaiah 3).

5. A MESSIAH WILL RESTORE THE KINGDOM OF ISRAEL AND BRING PEACE ON EARTH.

The word *Messiah* comes from the Hebrew word *maschiach*, which means "anointed one." In Old Testament times, anointment was the ritual in which a king was touched with a drop of holy oil as a sign that he enjoyed God's blessing. (The word "ointment" in English comes from the same root.) Several important passages in the books of Isaiah, Jeremiah, and Ezekiel point to a time when an "anointed one"—a descendant of the House of David—will end the period of exile and bring about an age of universal peace and justice.

It is at this point that Jewish and Christian interpretations diverge. Jewish tradition has usually seen the Messiah as an earthly king who, through conquest or some special act of righteousness, would restore Jewish rule in Israel and bring peace on earth. Christian tradition, on the other hand, maintains that Jesus of Nazareth fulfilled all the messianic prophecies of the Hebrew Bible. Much Christian interpretation views the Old Testament mainly as a preparation for the coming of Christ.

POINT OF VIEW

It's easy to see that the prophetic books of the Old Testament have a point of view. In a narrow sense, the viewpoint represented in each prophetic book is that of the prophet himself. But in a broader sense, in each of these books you can hear a prophet, speaking for God, tell the people that God has punished or will punish them for their wickedness and will redeem them if they repent. The central message is that there is an unbreakable connection between the evil that people do and the misfortunes that befall them, and between the good things that people do and the rewards they receive. An even broader message is that the events of history are not just random happenings: they follow a pattern, they convey a meaning, they reveal God's will.

Conflicting Viewpoints

But what *is* the meaning of history? On this question, the writers of the Bible do not seem to have shared the same point of view. For example, a critical question in the history of the ancient Hebrews was whether Israel should have a king. Throughout most of the twelfth and eleventh centuries B.C., the Hebrews were a loose confederation of tribes ruled by "judges," who were not jurists but charismatic leaders. The main argument against having an earthly king was that Israel was already under the protection of the Almighty. When Samuel, a judge and prophet, tells the Lord that the people are demanding a king of their own, he receives this answer:

> Hearken unto the voice of the people in all that they say unto thee: for they have not rejected thee, but they have rejected Me, that I should not reign over them.
>
> (1 Samuel 8:7)

By the time of David, however, the monarchy had become so strong that the king was regarded by many as the embodiment of God's will. Thus, those who supported David and his successors wrote of the period of the judges, when Israel had no king, as a time of anarchy and disorder. On the other hand, those who, echoing the views of the prophets, denounced the later rulers as corrupt and faithless tended to yearn for the time when Yahweh, fittingly, was Israel's true king. Both these strands run through the historical books, and the conflict between the positive and negative views of kingship underlies the treatment of heroes like David and Solomon as great but seriously flawed men.

On other questions, too, the Old Testament does not speak with a single voice. The Deuteronomic belief that obedience to God will invariably be rewarded is challenged in the books of Job and Ecclesiastes. The message of such writings as Ezra and Nehemiah is that the Hebrews must take pains to separate themselves from all foreign influences. The books of Ruth and Jonah, on the other hand, suggest that Jews can learn from non-Jews and that the lives of all people are precious to God.

The Critical Response

The nineteenth-century German critics of the Old Testament seized on conflicts such as these as evidence that parts of the Hebrew Bible were written by different hands at different times. The conflicting points of view, they held, reflected Israel's changing view of itself over the centuries. You might say they regarded the Old Testament as a kind of diary of the Jewish people. If you have ever kept a diary, you know how your outlook can change from day to day with a change in the weather, the swing of a grade, a family argument, the making or breaking of a friendship. As you read the Old Testament, observe carefully how the Bible's view of the Hebrew kings, priests, and people changes as Israel rides the roller coaster of history from slavery to empire, from exile to redemption.

LITERARY FORMS, STYLES, AND TECHNIQUES

Trying to describe the writing style of the Old Testament is like trying to describe the contents of your local library—the style varies from book to book, sometimes even from chapter to chapter and verse to verse. In fact, the Hebrew Bible has been compared to a library, consisting as it does of writings by different hands in different forms at different times.

Narrative Styles

One biblical form that should be very familiar to you is that of the chronicle, written in a kind of "and this happened . . . and that happened . . ." style. In the following example from the book of

Joshua (3:1–3), each *and* has been italicized to emphasize the repetitive pattern:

> *And* Joshua rose early in the morning; *and* they removed from Shittim, *and* came to Jordan, he *and* all the children of Israel, *and* lodged there before they passed over.
>
> *And* it came to pass after three days, that the officers went through the host;
>
> *And* they commanded the people, . . .

The books of Joshua, 1 and 2 Samuel, and 1 and 2 Kings are written entirely in this historical style, but the same kind of chronicle shows up in many other places. An extreme case can be found in the long lists of generations between Adam and Noah and between Noah and Abraham (Genesis 5, 10, 11). If you've ever told or heard someone else telling a long and oft-repeated story by saying "and then I did this . . . and then I did that . . . ," you'll understand why scholars see in this repetitive style the signs of a long oral tradition. Such genealogies and chronicles were passed down orally from parents to children for centuries before the Hebrews had a written language. (Remember that while Abraham probably lived about 2000 B.C. and the Exodus took place before 1200 B.C., the oldest known Hebrew inscription dates from the tenth century B.C.)

The chronicle is only one of many kinds of writing in the Old Testament. A common style in the Pentateuch is the law code, recognizable in the King James Version by "thou shalt . . . thou shalt not . . ." and in more modern translations by "you shall . . . you shall not. . . ." Interwoven with the historical and legal materials of the Pentateuch are beautiful descriptions of natural creation, realistic depictions of family quarrels, dramatic encounters among the patriarchs and between individual patriarchs and their God, and poetry of rare joy and triumph.

The Books and Their Forms

The Book of Isaiah combines moral sermonizing with inspirational poetry of the highest order, and the Book of Jeremiah mixes historical narrative and political commentary with poetry that is at times anguished and introspective. One book of the Old Testament, the Book of Psalms, consists wholly of poems directed to God. The Song of Solomon (also called Song of Songs) is an anthology of exotic love poetry, lush and sensuous in its imagery (2:1–4):

> I am the rose of Sharon, and the lily of the valleys.
>   As the lily among thorns, so is my love among the daughters.
>   As the apple tree among the trees of the wood, so is my beloved among the sons. I sat down under his shadow with great delight, and his fruit was sweet to my taste.
>   He brought me to the banqueting house, and his banner over me was love.

The Book of Lamentations, on the other hand, consists of songs of grief and mourning. The Book of Proverbs, an example of the Bible's "wisdom literature," is a collection of essays and sayings probably used as a kind of textbook of good behavior. As you read these sayings, some of which should already be familiar to you, notice how the many different kinds of parallelism in the prose carry the meaning forward.

Remarkable, too, are the books of Esther, Job, and Jonah, tightly organized works that can be read almost like a novel or short story. Consider, for example, in Jonah, the way the character of the prophet (who is chosen by God but tries to flee his mission) contrasts with the people of Nineveh (who are condemned by God but quickly embrace repentance and salvation). Just as the phrase "the presence of the Lord" recurs at key points in Jonah as a signal in following the story, so the phrase "and the Lord was with . . . " appears in the historical books whenever the Old Testament wishes to foreshadow a character's success.

Because of the variety of forms and styles, there is no single way to read the Bible. Different books must be read in different ways, using different tools of literary analysis.

TRANSLATIONS AND EDITIONS

In all human history, no book has been so widely read as the Bible. By the mid-1980s, the Bible had been translated, in whole or in part, into about 1800 languages and dialects. Books of the Bible have appeared in some 300 different English-language versions, ranging from the most scholarly translations to condensed or simplified texts and popular paraphrases.

The King James Version

Of all the translations of the entire Bible into English, none has had greater impact than the King James Version, which was published in the early seventeenth century, in the age of Shakespeare. Under the sponsorship of the English king James I, a team of 54 scholars, working in separate groups at Cambridge, Oxford, and Westminster, drew on Hebrew as well as Greek and Latin sources in order to produce a translation that would convey in English the rhythm and power of the Old Testament original. Upon publication, the King James text became the "Authorized" version, to be read in Anglican churches. Many editions of the King James translation have been printed, including the notorious "Wicked Bible" (1631), from which the word *not* in "Thou shalt not commit adultery" (Exodus 20:14) was mistakenly omitted; the error cost the printers a £300 fine.

Other English Translations

The King James Version was not the first Bible in English. The earliest complete English translation, the Lollard Bible, appeared in the fourteenth century; another reformist translation was produced in the 1530s by William Tyndale, a follower of Martin Luther. Subsequent translations in the sixteenth and early seventeenth centuries reflected the splintering of Christendom as a result of the Reformation. A Calvinist version, the Geneva Bible, appeared in 1560; an Anglican translation, the Bishops' Bible, in 1568; and the Douay version, a translation prepared by English Catholic émigrés, in 1609.

The language of the King James Version was old-fashioned even in its own time, and although its influence on the development of English literature has been profound, its use in worship services has steadily diminished. Our own century has brought a tremendous new burst of biblical translation. There are several reasons for this. First, the English language has changed—a change you become very much aware of when trying to understand *King Lear* and *Macbeth*, both written while the King James translation was under way. Second, biblical criticism and archaeology (including the discovery in 1947 of the Dead Sea Scrolls) have offered translators new tools for understanding the original texts.

Third, a new spirit of cooperation between Christians and Jews and among the various branches of Christendom has inspired scholars of different faiths to work with and learn from each other. Appearing in recent decades have been the Revised Standard Version (1946–52), based on the American Standard Version (1901) and the King James; the Jerusalem Bible (1966), representing an English translation of the French Dominican version; the New American Bible (1970), another Roman Catholic translation; the interfaith Anchor Bible, a multivolume translation and commentary whose publication began in 1964; and a three-volume translation of the Holy Scriptures sponsored by the Jewish Publication Society of America (1962–82).

Translation as Interpretation

Even when it includes no specific commentary, each translation is an interpretation. The translator's choice of one word over another can have an important effect on the meaning of a passage. Consider, for example, the sixth of the Ten Commandments (Exodus 20:13), translated in the King James Version of 1611 as "Thou shalt not kill." This commandment has been cited at various times as an argument against capital punishment—the death penalty—and in support of pacifism, or the refusal to take life under any circumstances. A more recent edition, called the New King James Version and published in 1982, renders the same text in a different way: "You shall not murder." A look at any good English dictionary will show you that while killing can mean the taking of *any* life for *any* reason, the word *murder* specifically means the unlawful killing of a human being. Now, you might still want to use Exodus 20:13 in arguing against the death penalty or in favor of pacifism, but the newer translation (which has much scholarly support) makes your task considerably more difficult.

Versions of the Twenty-third Psalm

No passage in the Old Testament is more familiar than the Twenty-third Psalm, which in the King James Version begins, "The Lord is my shepherd." As you read the translations that follow—only a few of many different versions that could have been cited—ask yourself how the translators' choice of form and diction affects your impression of the passage:

> *Psalms of Sir Philip Sidney and the Countess of Pembroke (c. 1599):*
> The Lord, the Lord my shepherd is,
>   And so can never I
>   Taste misery.
> He rests me in green pasture his:
>   By waters still, and sweet
>   He guides my feet.
> He me revives: leads me the way,
>   Which righteousness doth take,
>   For his name's sake.

> *Douay Bible (1609):*
> The Lord ruleth me: and I shall want nothing.
>   He hath set me in a place of pasture.
> He hath brought me up, on the water of refreshment: he hath converted my soul.
> He hath led me on the paths of justice, for his own name's sake.

> *King James Version (1611):*
> The Lord is my shepherd; I shall not want.
> He maketh me to lie down in green pastures: he leadeth me beside the still waters.
> He restoreth my soul: he leadeth me in the paths of righteousness for his name's sake.

Bay Psalm Book (1620):
The Lord to me a shepherd is,
   want therefore shall not I,
He in the folds of tender grass,
   doth cause me down to lie:
To waters calm me gently leads,
   restore my soul doth he:
He doth in paths of righteousness:
   for his name's sake lead me.

Revised Standard Version (1952):
The Lord is my shepherd, I shall not want;
   he makes me lie down in green pastures.
He leads me beside still waters;
   he restores my soul.
He leads me in paths of righteousness
   for his name's sake.

Jerusalem Bible (1966):
Yahweh is my shepherd,
   I lack nothing.
To the waters of repose he leads me:
   there he revives my soul.
He guides me by paths of virtue
   for the sake of his name.

Anchor Bible (1966):
Yahweh is my shepherd,
   I shall not lack.
In green meadows he will make me lie down:
Near tranquil waters he will guide me,
   to refresh my being,
He will lead me into luxuriant pastures,
   as befits his name.

SUBSEQUENT INFLUENCE

What if the Old Testament had never been written?

Suppose all record of the life and thought of the Hebrew people were suddenly to disappear. You travel to Italy to savor the masterworks of Michelangelo, but his magnificent sculptures of Moses and David are absent, and there are spaces in the Sistine Chapel frescoes where Adam and the Hebrew prophets were shown. In London, scheduled performances of Handel's *Messiah* and *Israel in Egypt* have been abruptly canceled. In Washington, D.C., at the Library of Congress, dozens of shelves are now empty, for not only have all the Bibles in all their translations vanished, but so have all editions of Milton's *Paradise Lost* and *Samson Agonistes*, Racine's *Esther* and *Athalie*, and Mann's *Joseph and His Brothers*.

The Old Testament and Western Culture

To measure the influence of the Old Testament, however, you need more than a brief listing of works of art, music, and literature on biblical themes. The plain truth is that the influence of the Old Testament in Western culture is incalculably vast. For a thousand years of European history, no one who could read at all was unfamiliar with the Bible in church Latin. During the fifteenth and sixteenth centuries, as printing technology developed, translations of the Bible into English, French, German, and other languages spread both literacy and new religious ideas.

No book has had such a distinguished international roster of translators. By far the most important German translator was the great Protestant reformer Martin Luther, whose edition (1522–34) influenced the development of the German language as profoundly as the King James Version shaped the growth of English. The King James translators were among the finest scholars of their age. Outstanding Jewish translators of the Old

Testament have included Moses Mendelssohn, a major figure of the eighteenth-century German enlightenment, and the twentieth-century German philosophers Martin Buber and Franz Rosenzweig.

The Old Testament Outlook

In dwelling on the history of the Old Testament as a book, we barely hint at how it has shaped our way of thinking. Without this record of the ancient Hebrew thought, there could be no Judaism; without Judaism (and its messianic beliefs), there could be no Christianity; without Judaism and Christianity, there could be no Islam. Without the Old Testament, the lives and beliefs of today's more than 1 billion Christians, 550 million Muslims, and 14 million Jews would be profoundly different. Nor would the difference be confined to religion, for religion has a profound influence on culture. The Sabbath in the Old Testament has become part of our weekend. The prophetic ideals of righteousness, justice, and peace find expression in our charitable agencies, court system, and the United Nations.

The Old Testament's uncompromising insistence on the supremacy of one God, one law, and one truth continues to shape our way of thinking about the world, even about science. (If you doubt this, ask yourself how advanced the science of meteorology would be if weather forecasting focused on the caprices of the sun-god, the rain-god, and Thor the thunder-maker.) Today, few scientists regard the Bible as an infallible guide to natural science; even so, the search for unified theories in cosmology, particle physics, biology, and other branches of science draws power from the ancient

Hebrew conviction that the universe follows a clear and consistent pattern that people were meant to understand. As Albert Einstein, the father of relativity theory, said, "I shall never believe that God plays dice with the world."

BOOKS OF THE OLD TESTAMENT

Genesis

Overview

"Genesis" comes from a Greek word meaning "origin" or "source"; the same root underlies the word "genetics," the science that probes the chemical origins of life. The book's name in Hebrew is *Bereshit* (the first word of the Genesis narrative), which means "In the beginning."

Traditionalists regard Genesis, the first book of the Pentateuch, as having been given directly by God to Moses at Mount Sinai. Biblical critics, on the other hand, hold that Genesis consists of a series of separate documents set down by the J, E, and P writers and woven together by an editor or editors around 400 B.C. (For an introduction to the critical theory and an indication of what the letters J, E, and P stand for, see "The Development of the Canon" in The Old Testament Background section.)

According to calculations made in the seventeenth century by the Irish archbishop James Ussher (and still included in many editions of the King James Bible), Genesis extends from the year 4004 B.C., when God created the world, to the death of Joseph in Egypt 2315 years later. Today, few commentators are as certain as Ussher was of the precision of biblical chronology. Most astronomers maintain that the universe is not thousands but *billions* of years old, and archaeological evidence indicates that humanlike creatures have roamed the earth for millions of years. Numerous attempts have been made, both in our own time and in preceding centuries, to harmonize the biblical account of Creation with scientific theories and discoveries. In recent decades, Christian fundamentalists have based a "creation science" on acceptance of the truth of the Bible as a scientific document. Many of the believing Christians and Jews who dispute the fundamentalist view regard the truths of the Bible not necessarily as scientific or historical truths but as *truths of faith*, basic to the Judeo-Christian view of life as an extension of God's creative power.

Not in dispute is the literary majesty of Genesis. In this one book are found accounts of God's awesome creative and destructive powers, the origins of the universe, the fashioning of the first man and the first woman, the beginnings of good and evil, the first followers of Yahweh, and the covenant between God and humankind. No book is more central to the development in Western culture of the meaning of good and evil and a sense of humanity's place in the world.

Creation and Destruction (Genesis 1:1—11:9)

In only a few pages, the Book of Genesis attempts to answer the most profound questions anyone can ask. Is there an order to the universe? Is there any power greater than ourselves? Where did humankind come from, and what is the purpose of life on earth? How did evil and suffering originate?

NOTE: A distinctive feature of Creation in the Book of Genesis is that it is *ex nihilo*—a Latin expression meaning "out of nothing." Before Creation, says Genesis 1:2, "the earth was without form, and void." Nothing is said of God's existence prior to Creation, nor is any reason given for this act.

The opening chapters of Genesis offer a blueprint for Creation, as God—here called Elohim—molds a formless and watery world into the environment familiar to our senses. (Mesopotamian myths also associate water with primeval chaos.) God's initial task is to create light and separate it from darkness, thereby making the *first* day. On the *second* day, God makes Heaven (also translated as the heavens, or sky); on the *third* day, Earth (or dry land), seas, and plants; on the *fourth* day, stars, sun, and moon; on the *fifth* day, creatures of the sea and sky; on the *sixth* day, creatures of the land, including man "in His own image." You may have noticed that after each of the first five days God examines His Creation and pronounces it "good," but on the sixth day—the day on which man and woman emerge—God calls His handiwork "very good" (1:31). The message, stated explicitly in 1:28–30, is that humanity represents the fulfillment of the creative design. Just as God has no rival as the shaping and controlling force in the universe, so humanity has no rival as ruler of the natural world. In Genesis 2:1–3, after six days of "making," God ceases His labors and sanctifies the *seventh* day as a day of rest.

NOTE: The English word "Sabbath," or seventh day, comes from the Hebrew "Shabbat," which itself stems from *shavat*, or "rest." The concept of a special day of refreshment or celebration may have its origin in the Babylonian *shapattu*, a once-a-month celebration of the full moon. However, the idea of a weekly day of rest—a day, moreover, that is as sacred as any of the days of active creation—seems wholly without precedent. Remembrance of the Sabbath is the only ritual specified in the Ten Commandments (Exodus 20:8–11).

Genesis 2:4 takes you right back to the beginning. Why does the Bible repeat the Creation story? As you read 2:4–25, try to keep clearly in mind the first version of Creation. Notice, for example, that in the first narrative, animals are created before human beings, but in the second version the animals are created for and named by man. In the first version, male and female are created together; in the second, the woman is fashioned from the man, to serve as a helper for him.

What do these differences mean? If you accept the idea that the Bible has several authors, this passage offers powerful support. God is referred to not as Elohim but as Yahweh Elohim (the Lord God) or Yahweh. The documentary hypothesis holds that the change of names and new order of Creation reflect a different tradition and a different author. According to this theory, the editor of the finished text, regarding the writings of both authors as sacred, simply placed them side by side, without attempting to harmonize their contradictions. Traditionalists answer this argument by maintaining that the two versions of Creation reflect different emphases. The first version, they say, reflects the nature of the world as it ought to be.

The second—including the subordination of woman to man, the disobedience of Adam and Eve, and the expulsion from paradise—reflect the world as it is.

NOTE: "Adam" and "Eve" look like personal names, and they are common as first names today, but they have hidden Hebrew meanings. "Adam" in the Hebrew original means "man" and is related to the word for "earth" or "dust" (see God's curse on Adam at 3:19). The name "Eve" comes from the Hebrew *chavah*, which means "mother of all living things."

The story of Adam and Eve's temptation and fall (2:15—3:24) is deceptively simple. God places Adam in the Garden of Eden and tells him that he is free to eat the fruit of every tree in the garden except one—the tree of the knowledge of good and evil. God warns him that the penalty for eating the fruit is death. One day a serpent appears before Eve, who has been told of God's warning. The serpent persuades Eve to taste the fruit, and she gives some of it to Adam. Adam and Eve then try to hide from God, but He finds them and, confirming their wrongdoing, punishes them and the serpent.

On the simplest level, this is a story of an angry parent punishing his disobedient children—a scene you have perhaps lived through when you sampled the cake that was reserved for guests, puffed on a forbidden cigarette, or stayed out too late on a date. But if you read this story really closely, you will find many problems—the same kinds of problems that have troubled commentators for more than 2000 years.

1.   Why was it wrong to eat from the tree of the knowledge of good and evil? One possible answer is that it was wrong simply because God said so. The fruit itself was not evil—only the eating of it in defiance of God's warning. Another explanation is that before eating the fruit, humanity was incapable of sinning. Once the fruit was eaten, however, people were for the first time aware of the difference between right and wrong, and thus capable of choosing evil; no longer innocent, Adam and Eve could no longer remain in paradise. A third answer is that God will accept no rivals. The serpent promises Eve that if she and Adam taste the fruit they "will be as gods, knowing good and evil." Eating the fruit means that Adam and Eve no longer wish to *serve* God but to *be* gods. (Remember this interpretation when you come to the Tower of Babel episode at 11:1–9.) A fourth possible answer connects the tasting of the fruit with the discovery of sexuality; evidence for this explanation is that Adam and Eve's first feelings after eating the fruit are nakedness and shame. After girls and boys become women and men, they cannot remain in the state of innocence the Garden of Eden represents.

2.   What are the consequences of Adam and Eve's disobedience? God's curses are explicit: the serpent will crawl on his belly and live in the dust; Eve will feel pain in childbirth and be ruled by her husband; Adam will have to work hard for a living until the day he dies; and Adam and Eve will be forever barred from the Garden of Eden. But what of the broader implications of this fall from grace?

Christian doctrine holds that because of the first fall, all human beings are tarnished with original sin. Only with the coming of Jesus Christ and through faith in the Redeemer can this stain be removed from one's soul. Judaism, on the other hand, denies that humanity is inherently stained. Instead, it emphasizes the importance of doing good deeds, of fulfilling the biblical commandments and avoiding evil impulses.

3. If God is omniscient, or all-knowing, then He must have known that Eve and Adam were going to eat the fruit. If so, why did He plant the forbidden tree in the garden? Moreover, why were Adam and Eve punished for a crime that was foreknown and foreordained—a crime that, seemingly, they had no choice but to commit? Such questions point to the central dilemma of reconciling the Old Testament concept of an omniscient and omnipotent (all-powerful) God with our strongly held belief in our own free will. Attempts to resolve this dilemma still play a vital role in Christian and Jewish writings on theology.

NOTE: Two symbols in the Eden story have also been variously interpreted. Many ancient Near Eastern myths portray serpents as opposing the will of the gods; late Hebrew and Christian writings identify the serpent with Satan, a devil figure. Grapes, figs, and citrons—products of the Mediterranean world—have all served in Jewish tradition as "fruits" of the tree of the knowledge of good and evil. Many Christian writers have regarded the forbidden fruit as an apple, in part because the Latin word for apple (*malus*) also means "bad."

The Bible offers a grim portrait of life between the expulsion from Eden and the coming of the patriarchs.

Adam and Eve have two sons: Cain, a farmer, and Abel, a shepherd. In time, each offers a sacrifice to the Lord, but Cain's sacrifice of crops is rejected, while Abel's offering of his choicest lambs is accepted. The text does not say exactly why God accepts one offering and not the other. Perhaps the fact that Abel offers the "firstlings" of his flock (4:4) is meant to show that his devotion to God is more sincere than Cain's. Or perhaps a bias toward animal sacrifice is the kind of favoritism a shepherd people (and many scholars believe the ancient Hebrews began as shepherds) would expect of their tribal deity. A third interpretation holds that God's reasons are often unfathomable, and that Cain is a tragic figure because he knows he has been rejected by God but cannot comprehend the reason for the rejection.

Enraged and jealous at the favored treatment his brother has received, Cain lures Abel out into a field and kills him. When the Lord asks Cain where Abel is, Cain answers, "Am I my brother's keeper?" (4:9). But God already knows what has happened. Notice that Cain's punishment for this first murder is like that of Adam and Eve for their first disobedience—banishment and a lifetime of shame and struggle.

NOTE: Favoritism shown to a younger son and the bitterness that results from such favoritism are

themes that recur often in Genesis. Watch for these
themes as you read of Ishmael and Isaac, Esau and
Jacob, and Joseph and his brothers.

The line of Adam extends not through Cain but
through a later son, Seth. After many generations
and many centuries, humanity has become completely corrupt. God regrets having made mankind
and resolves to destroy his Creation. Only Noah,
"a just man and perfect in his generations" (6:9),
will be allowed to survive the coming flood and,
by building a great ark, preserve a remnant of animal life. This great vessel, about 450 feet long and
45 feet high (assuming that 1 cubit = 18 inches),
takes Noah about 100 years to build, and he is 600
years old when the deluge begins. The rains last
40 days, but the flood itself lasts almost a year.
When, at last, the flood waters have completely
receded, Noah makes a sacrifice to God, who
pledges never again to destroy the world because
of human wickedness.

There are many levels to the Noah story. On a
simple level, you can find in the Noah story an
ancient attempt to explain why floods and rain-
bows happen. The fact that flood stories appear in
several Mesopotamian documents, notably the *Gilgamesh Epic*, has encouraged some critics to view
this story as little more than a Hebrew version of
an old Near Eastern myth. Some traditionalists, on
the other hand, look to the appearance of similar
stories in other sources as confirmation of the historical truth of the biblical narrative. Many commentators focus on the differences between the
Gilgamesh and Noah accounts. While the Near
Eastern myths dwell on the role of gods and heroes,

the Old Testament makes no attempt to glorify or deify Noah; he is a good man of his time, but no god. Moreover, the coming of the flood and the agreement made by God with Noah after the deluge have a moral dimension wholly lacking in the Mesopotamian tales. Polytheists often thought of natural disasters as the results of quarrels among the gods; the monotheistic Hebrews thought of such calamities as God's punishment for human wrongdoing.

NOTE: Have you begun to mark your text for basic themes and concepts? If so, be sure to mark Noah as a *prophet*, because he acts on God's behalf. Be sure also to note the pledge God makes to Noah as one of a series of *convenants* between God and His people.

The theme of divine punishment for human wrongdoing makes another appearance in the story of the Tower of Babel (11:1–9), which also represents an attempt to explain the dispersion of peoples and profusion of languages in the world. There is general agreement among scholars that the tower that threatened to "reach unto heaven" is a Babylonian ziggurat, perhaps the Temple of Marduk in Babylon; the word *Babel* is itself linked both to Babylon and to the resultant "babble" of languages that God created to confound the tower builders' aspirations. Intepreters differ on the question of whether the builders are punished because of their aspirations to godhood and unlimited pride in human endeavor, or because a jealous God feared that the tower would be used to launch a physical assault on heaven, or because the ancient Hebrews saw this ancient story as a way to show their God's supremacy to the gods of Babylon.

The Covenants of Abraham (Genesis 11:10—22:24)

The first ten chapters of Genesis deal with the early history of all humanity. With the appearance of Abraham in chapter 11, however, the Bible begins to concern itself primarily with the history of the Hebrew people. After listing the ancestors of Abraham (at first called Abram, "the father is exalted"), the Bible announces the first of God's great commandments and promises to the Hebrew patriarch (12:1–3):

> Get thee out of thy country, and from thy kindred, and from thy father's house, unto a land that I will shew thee:
> And I will make of thee a great nation, and I will bless thee, and make thy name great; and thou shalt be a blessing.

Why did God choose Abraham and not someone else? Genesis, remarkably, is silent on this question, offering no special praise for Abraham at the outset. Some commentators take this silence to mean that Abraham is chosen through no merit of his own but rather through God's grace, to fulfill the divine purpose. Others hold that elsewhere in Genesis, Abraham shows the special qualities that led God to single him out. Within the Jewish tradition, many folktales attest to Abraham's early rejection of idolatry and adherence to the one God. An attempt to join the two interpretations leads to the idea that God chose Abraham, but that Abraham also chose God by consenting to obey God's commands.

At the age of seventy-five, Abraham leaves the land of his ancestors in Mesopotamia and journeys with his wife Sarah (at first called Sarai, a dialectal version of the Hebrew word for "princess"), his nephew Lot, and all the rest of their household to the land of Canaan, which God then identifies as His gift to Abraham and his descendants—the Promised Land. After a brief sojourn in Egypt, they return to Canaan, where Lot and Abraham go their separate ways. Lot settles in the east, in the plain of the Jordan River, but Abraham remains in Canaan. There God renews his covenant with Abraham, promising the old man—who is still childless—that his seed, his descendants, will be as numberless as the dust of the earth and that they will have their own land to live in (13:14–18).

Several years later, Abraham finally begets his first child, Ishmael, traditionally regarded as the patriarch of the Arab people. The mother of this child is not Sarah but Hagar, an Egyptian servant. Later, after Sarah bears Abraham a son of her own (Isaac), Hagar and Ishmael will be cast out at Sarah's insistence. Before Sarah conceives, however, she and Abraham are visited by God, who restates His earlier pledges to the patriarch and, as a sign of the covenant between them, commands Abraham, all the males of his household, and all his male descendants to be circumcised (17:10–14).

NOTE: Circumcision—surgical removal of the foreskin covering the head of the penis—is the sign of the Abrahamic covenant, just as the rainbow is the sign of God's covenant with Noah. The Hebrews did not invent circumcision, which was widely practiced in the Near East in biblical times. What the Hebrews did was to change the practice from a rite of sexual initiation, performed at puberty, to a ritual of religious commitment, performed when a boy is eight days old.

Of all God's promises to Abraham, the one the patriarch and his wife find most difficult to believe is the pledge that Abraham, now ninety-nine years of age, and Sarah, at age ninety, will conceive a son, Isaac ("he laughs"), with whom God will renew His covenant. Genesis tells us that both Abraham and Sarah laugh at this prophecy, prompting God to rebuke them, asking, "Is any thing too hard for the Lord?" (18:14). This idea that the Lord can overcome all obstacles is a recurrent theme in the Old Testament; look for it, for example, when you read Numbers 13–14 and the Book of Judges.

Notice that Genesis does not portray Abraham and Sarah as the passive instruments of the divine will. They show very human weaknesses and doubts, and an evident willingness to question— even quarrel with—God. When God reveals to Abraham His intention to destroy the wicked cities of Sodom and Gomorrah, the patriarch questions God closely, pleading with Him to change His plans for the sake of the few righteous people who might live there (18:23–32). This dialogue, which reveals both God's mercy and Abraham's integrity, gives no help at all to the unsalvageable Sodom and Gomorrah, which are consumed by "brimstone and fire" (19:24), with Lot and his two daughters the lone survivors. Lot's wife, also given the chance to escape, hesitates and is turned into a "pillar of salt" (19:26).

The image of the pillar of salt, which surely belongs to the world of folklore and legend, forever defines Lot's wife, whose name is never given in the Bible. But even much more familiar characters, with well-known names, tend to be defined in the popular imagination by simple words and concepts. If you are at all familiar with the Old Testament, you probably associate law with Moses, wisdom with Solomon, a slingshot with David. Abraham, on the other hand, issues no law codes, tries no cases, commands no armies. He too is a hero, but a hero of faith.

Just what it means to be a hero of faith Genesis 21–22 now makes clear. If you have not already read these chapters, do so now. No summary or commentary can hope to convey the disturbing power of Genesis 22:1–19, and if you do not read what the Bible says of Abraham and his son Isaac, you cheat yourself of a story that lies at the heart of Old Testament ethics and spirituality.

A brief review of the narrative. Isaac is born, as God foretold. His circumcision, followed by Ishmael's banishment, makes Isaac Abraham's true heir. Suddenly, however, God commands Abraham to ascend one of the mountains of Moriah, there to offer Isaac as a sacrifice to the Lord. Abraham, making no protest, does as he is told. He binds Isaac, places him upon an altar, and is about to slay him when, just as suddenly, an angel of the Lord orders him to stop. A ram found caught in a nearby thicket is offered as a substitute sacrifice, and father and son descend the mountain and head back home.

NOTE: Responding to Abraham's show of steadfast faith, God reaffirms the covenant, this time in
terms even more expansive than before. Compare
the images of stars and sand at 22:17 with those of
the stars at 15:5 and the "dust of the earth" at
13:16.

Looked at closely, the *Akedah*—the Hebrew term
for the binding of Isaac—raises some very profound questions.

1. What do you learn about God from what He
says and does in this story? Why does God need
to test Abraham's faith, and what kind of God asks
a righteous man for this kind of sacrifice? Does an
all-knowing God test Abraham only because He is
sure the patriarch will pass the test? Or is the test
designed to show Abraham that just as God can
do anything, even the "impossible" (remember how
old Isaac's parents are when the child is born!), so
He is prepared to ask humanity to do the impossible in His service?

2. What does the test reveal about the character of Abraham? Why does Abraham dispute with
God about the fate of Sodom and Gomorrah but
not about the command to sacrifice his own son?
One possible answer to this second question is that
when God announces the cities' planned destruction, He is sharing a confidence with Abraham,
not making a commandment; plans can be discussed and revised, but a divine order cannot be.
Christianity has laid great stress on the binding of
Isaac both because it shows Abraham's justifica-

tion by faith (and not just good deeds) and because the offering of Isaac prefigures in the New Testament the crucifixion of Jesus, God's only begotten son.

3. What does the story say about the society of the time? Notice that Sarah, the boy's mother, barely figures in this story, nor does Isaac raise any protest. In the patriarchal world of the Old Testament, Abraham's power as head of the household is unquestioned. (Compare's Lot's offer to protect his guests by offering up his daughters at 19:8.) In this world, also, the gods were thought to demand human sacrifice; the fact that in the Akedah story the sacrifice is commanded but not carried out can be seen as the Hebrews' rejection of the practice.

4. What lessons does the binding of Isaac hold for faith and ethics? In *Fear and Trembling*, the nineteenth-century Danish philosopher Søren Kierkegaard asked his readers to consider what would happen if some dutiful churchgoer, after hearing his pastor preach the virtues of Abraham, went home and sacrificed his own child at the urging of some heavenly voice? Imagine, said Kierkegaard, the outrage the preacher and community would heap on this person for doing what we so comfortably praise Abraham for doing—following without hesitation the dictates of his faith. Is the kind of faith that Abraham shows appropriate only to an age of miracles? How, in our modern world, can we distinguish the calling of genuine faith from a murderous lunacy?

From Jacob to Joseph (Genesis 23:1—50:26)

Chapters 23–25 mark the passing of generations. Sarah dies, and a marriage with a non-Canaanite,

Rebekah, is arranged for Isaac. At 25:7–8 comes the death of Abraham himself, at the ripe age of 175, but not before he takes another wife, Keturah, and has six more children. The genealogies at 25:2–4 are the Bible's way of accounting for the manifold tribes of the ancient Near East. As for the exceptionally long lifetimes of the patriarchs and their biblical forerunners, some commentators have attempted to second-guess the biblical chronology, speculating, for example, that one of our years might count for two in Genesis (thus Abraham would die at the age of 87½ rather than 175). Other writers accept the legendary qualities of the narrative, already suggested at 6:4, "There were giants in the earth in those days." Probably the ancient Israelites, who did not believe in life after death, thought of long life and prosperity as expressions of the Lord's blessings.

Although God appears before Isaac to reaffirm the Abrahamic covenant, Isaac plays a much less significant role in Genesis than does his father. Attention soon shifts to Isaac and Rebekah's twin sons, the hairy Esau (ancestor of the Edomites) and the smooth-skinned Jacob. Although Esau is the first to emerge from the womb, all signs indicate that Jacob will inherit the birthright that is customarily the firstborn's due. One day, when Esau comes home famished, Jacob seizes the advantage by exacting from Esau a pledge to give up his birthright—that is, his inheritance—in exchange for a bowl of lentil soup. The rivalry between the two sons splits the family down the middle, with Isaac taking Esau's part and Rebekah favoring Jacob. This saga of jealousy and domestic intrigue reaches a climax when Isaac, old and nearly blind, calls for Esau, a hunter, to make him a dish of his favorite meat stew and so receive Isaac's deathbed blessing. While Esau is out hunting venison for the stew, Rebekah connives to make her own stew, dresses Jacob in animal skins to make him seem hairy, and sends Jacob in to his father to receive the blessing under false pretenses. The ruse works, but Esau, furious at being cheated, swears to kill Jacob once Isaac has died and the period of mourning is over. Rebekah then warns Jacob, who, before fleeing the household, again receives a blessing from his father. Notice that this time the blessing is given by Isaac knowingly and is therefore untainted by deception.

NOTE: Does Esau get a raw deal? Commentators have long assumed that Esau, who so readily gives up his birthright, thereby proves himself unworthy of it. On the other hand, Jacob's evident ambition for the birthright is no virtue, nor does the Bible commend the deceit by which he gets it. (This is the old question of whether the ends justify the means.) Many writers have focused on Esau's uncivilized qualities and on the animal appetites he feeds in Isaac.

The story of Jacob in exile mingles the most miraculous visions with another round of domestic entanglements. On the way toward Laban's house at Haran, Jacob has a dream in which he sees angels of God ascending and descending a ladder or stairway that stretches from earth all the way to heaven; this vision is the occasion for yet another renewal and extension of the Abrahamic covenant (28:13–15). At Haran, Jacob takes not one wife but two—first the unwanted Leah, through the trickery of Jacob's uncle Laban, then Rachel, Leah's younger sister and Jacob's true love. Much of Jacob's stay with Laban can be seen as an essay in theft and deception, extending the theme introduced with Isaac's falsely procured blessing. Laban repeatedly cheats Jacob, and when after twenty years Jacob flees Haran with Leah and Rachel and all their children, Rachel secretly takes Laban's household idols with her and then, through another deception, prevents her father from discovering the theft. Why does Rachel take the idols? Perhaps as good-luck objects, or as a sign that Laban no longer has any power over Jacob's household. Unquestionably, she is disloyal to her father, and Jacob's oath at 31:32—that whoever stole the idols shall not live—bears bitter fruit when Rachel dies in childbirth several years later. (For another example of a rash oath with tragic consequences, see the story of Jephthah and his daughter at Judges 11:30–40.)

In the interim, Jacob has a second visionary experience (32:22–32). While on his way from Laban's toward an uncertain reunion with Esau, Jacob is met at the ford of the river Jabbok by a mysterious figure. The two wrestle until daybreak, with the wounded Jacob refusing to let go until the stranger gives him a blessing. Not only does the stranger bless Jacob, but he also gives him a new name, Israel, meaning (according to various commentators) "one who strives with God" or "may God rule." From this episode come the terms *Israelite*, *children of Israel* (that is, the descendants of Jacob), *land of Israel*, and *State of Israel*.

Who is this mysterious stranger who wrestles with Jacob? A river demon? An angel of heaven?

God Himself? Jacob's guilty conscience at having cheated Esau? The darker side of his own nature? Whatever your opinion, you can be sure the arguments over the precise identity of Jacob's adversary will not soon be resolved. There is, however, a general agreement that the struggle serves to purify Jacob/Israel, making possible at long last the reconciliation with Esau (33:1–17).

You might think that freedom from Laban and resolution of the quarrel with Esau would usher in a period of tranquility in Jacob's life. But that is not what happens. Like Adam, Abraham, and Isaac before him, Jacob must now endure the consequences of jealousy, rivalry, and deceit within his own household. Chapter 34 opens with the rape of Jacob's daughter Dinah by Shechem, the son of Hamor the Hivite. Shechem and Hamor then come to Jacob and his sons, offering to pay any bride-price so long as Dinah can become Shechem's wife. Jacob's sons tell Hamor and Shechem that there can be no intermarriage unless Shechem and his people allow themselves to be circumcised. Shechem gladly accepts the offer, but on the third day after the mass circumcision, before the wounds have had a chance to heal, Dinah's brothers Simeon and Levi treacherously kill the men and seize all their wealth, wives, and children.

NOTE: Genesis does not excuse the rape of Dinah, nor does it deny the right of Dinah's family to seek vengeance. But when Jacob's sons induce the men of Shechem to circumcise themselves, they are wrongfully using the sign of God's covenant with Abraham as a tactic to gain blood revenge.

Chapter 35 brings the deaths of Rachel and Isaac, and chapter 36 lists the descendants of Esau (that is, the ancestors of the Edomites). In chapter 37, the tale of family conflict resumes, with the familiar story of Joseph and his brothers. Genesis offers many reasons why the other brothers are jealous of him: he is the child of Jacob's old age, his father's favorite; Jacob has given him a "coat of many colours" (in one modern translation, an "ornamented tunic"); he tattles on his brothers' misdeeds; and he has dreams in which, symbolically, his father and brothers bow down to him. The brothers seize the boy Joseph, strip off his coat, cast him into a pit, and for twenty pieces of silver sell him into slavery in Egypt. Then they dip the coat in goat blood and bring it to Jacob, who concludes that an evil beast has eaten his beloved son.

"And the Lord was with Joseph," says Genesis 39:2, introducing the remarkable series of events that raise Joseph, now a mature man, from slavery to vast political and economic power. (The phrase "And the Lord was with . . . " recurs in the Old Testament in connection with such important figures as Moses, Joshua, and David. It's a literary device—a sign that good things are in store for this character and, if the character is a leader, that good things are in store for his people.) Falsely accused of adultery with the wife of Potiphar, his master, Joseph is cast into prison. There he is treated kindly and earns a reputation as an interpreter of dreams. When Pharaoh, the ruler of Egypt, has two dreams that none of his wise men can interpret, Joseph is called from prison. He tells Pharaoh that both dreams—one of cattle, the other of corn—signify that seven years of bountiful harvests will be followed by seven years of famine. The devastating

effects of famine can be avoided, says Joseph, only
if Pharaoh appoints someone to see that the sur-
pluses from the good years are safely stockpiled
and then distributed during the lean years that follow. Impressed by this wisdom, which Joseph attributes to Yahweh, Pharaoh appoints Joseph, then
only thirty years old, to oversee all Egyptian agriculture. He executes his office so well that when
famine does arrive, Egypt has enough grain to feed
its people and sell at a profit to other afflicted lands.
Meanwhile, in famine-stricken Canaan, Jacob sends
ten of his remaining sons—all except Benjamin—
to Egypt to buy grain. When they come to Joseph,
he recognizes them but they do not recognize him.

Why don't Joseph's brothers know who he is?
One answer is that two decades have passed,
during which Joseph has passed from adoles-
cence to mature manhood. A second answer is
that when his brothers last saw him, he was on
his way into slavery. How could they have imag-
ined that this young Hebrew would rise to a position of power in Egypt second only to that of
Pharaoh himself? Moreover, by the time the
brothers go down to Egypt, Joseph has become
fully assimilated. He speaks like an Egyptian,
dresses like an Egyptian, and has an Egyptian wife
and an Egyptian name.

NOTE: Joseph's new name, Zaphenath-paneah,
can be translated as "revealer of secret things."
Notice how, in the chapters that follow, Joseph's
boyhood dreams are fulfilled, just as all the dreams
he interprets in Egypt have already come to pass.
In its treatment of dreams as revelations of the

future, the Bible adheres to prevailing sentiment in ancient Egypt and elsewhere.

Joseph's brothers appear before him at 42:6, but Joseph keeps his true identity secret from them until 45:3. The intervening chapters detail an elaborate plot through which Joseph, by testing and humiliating his former tormentors, seeks to work out his simultaneous desires for revenge and reconciliation. The key event of Joseph's scheme is the false imprisonment of Benjamin, Jacob's new favorite, on charges that recall Rachel's crime. Not until Judah offers himself as a slave instead of Benjamin—an offer that shows the brothers' growing love for their father and for each other—can the test end and Joseph reveal himself. In time, Jacob himself moves down to Egypt, and at 46:29 father and son have a tearful reunion. The Book of Genesis ends with Jacob's blessing two of Joseph's sons, Ephraim and Manasseh; with the testament of Jacob, embodying his judgments on all his sons (a passage attributed by modern scholars to the period of the Judges, around the eleventh century B.C.); and with the deaths of Jacob and Joseph in Egypt.

Exodus

Overview

Exodus—a Greek word for "going out"—is the second book of the Old Testament. (In Hebrew the book is called *Shemot*, or "Names," from verse 1:1, "Now these are the names. . . .") Orthodox Jews and fundamentalist Christians believe that Exo-

dus, like Genesis and the other three books of the
Pentateuch, was given by God directly to Moses
on Mount Sinai. Some critics regard Exodus as an
intricate amalgam of texts from the J, E, and P
writers. According to this view, the E writer, or
Elohist, is solely or primarily responsible for chapters 20–23, including the Ten Commandments. To
P, the priestly writer, belongs sole or primary credit
for chapters 25–31 and 35–40, which deal with the
building of the Tabernacle, the tent-sanctuary in
which the presence of God was to abide among
the people.

The Book of Exodus falls into two main sections.
Chapters 1–18 are in the narrative style of Genesis
and describe the Hebrews' enslavement in and liberation from Egypt. Chapters 19–40 record the giving of the Law to Moses at Sinai. Except for the
episode of the golden calf (chapters 32–34), this
second section is cast in the legal style that dominates the remainder of the Pentateuch.

From Slavery to Sinai (1:1—18:27)

The Bible traces with swift strokes the descent of
the Hebrews from power and prosperity under Joseph to bondage under Pharaoh (1:8):

> Now there arose up a new king over Egypt,
> which knew not Joseph.

Pharaoh's fear, according to Exodus, is that the
Hebrews have grown so powerful and so numerous that they pose a threat to the integrity and
stability of the state. To suppress this threat, Pharaoh reduces the Israelites to bondage, makes their
work conditions intolerable, and then orders that
every Hebrew male child be killed at birth. When

the courageous midwives refuse to perform this act of cruelty, the king decrees that every Hebrew male infant be drowned in the Nile.

This biblical account of the persecution of the Israelites has not been confirmed, but scholars have long known that the period from about 1750 to 1500 B.C. was a time of great upheaval in Egypt. During most of this period, Egypt was ruled by the Hyksos, invaders from Palestine. Historians caution against making any simple equation between Hyksos and Hebrews. Nevertheless, it is surely consistent with the biblical account to assume that the fall of the Hyksos around 1500 B.C. was in some way connected with the drastic decline in the fortunes of the Hebrews, who were, like the Hyksos, Semites from Canaan. These dates are consistent with a biblical chronology that places Joseph's rise to power at around 1700 B.C. and the departure from Egypt at between 1250 B.C. and 1200 B.C., during the reign of the pharaoh Raamses II. (Some history books spell this name Ramses, Rameses, or Ramesses.)

At Exodus 2:1 attention shifts to Moses, a Levite infant saved from death in the Nile when his mother sets him adrift in a basket of bulrushes and he is discovered and raised by Pharaoh's own daughter. Critics of the Bible have noted that infanticide was alien to Egyptian but not to Mesopotamian tradition. They point to the Akkadian legend of King Sargon as the main source of the story of Moses' birth:

> My priestly mother conceived me, in secret she
>   bore me.
> She set me in a basket of rushes, with bitumen
>   she sealed my lid.

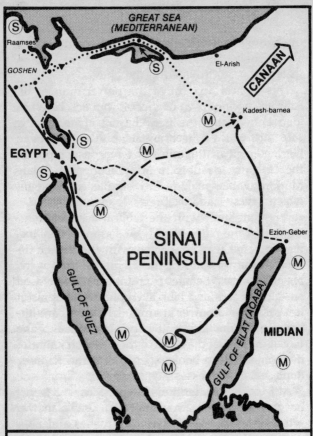

Major theories on the Israelites' route from Egypt to Kadesh-barnea;
in addition to the routes, the major sites are given according to
various theories.

Supposed Routes of the Exodus

••••• NORTHERN ROUTE	Proposed locations of Sea of Reeds ⓈS
– – CENTRAL ROUTE 1	
- - - CENTRAL ROUTE 2	Proposed locations for Mount Sinai ⓂM
—— SOUTHERN ROUTE	

She cast me into the river which rose not over
    me.
The river bore me up and carried me to Akki,
    the drawer of water.

Raised in the royal household, Moses becomes
an outlaw when he kills an Egyptian overseer he
sees mistreating a Hebrew slave. Moses flees to
the land of the Midianites and marries Zipporah,
the daughter of Jethro, a Midianite priest. While
Moses is tending Jethro's flocks, he comes to Mount
Horeb, where God, speaking from a burning bush,
calls upon Moses to serve as His messenger in setting the children of Israel free. As you read this
important scene (3:1—4:18), you should watch for
at least three things. The first is the theme of the
reluctant prophet, who cannot understand why God
has chosen him and who regards his calling as at
least as much a burden as an honor (compare Jeremiah and Jonah). The second is the theme of the
flawed hero, which appears here as a lack of elo-
quence or a speech defect (4:10) that makes Moses
doubt his ability to lead his people. The third theme
is heralded by Moses' fear that the Israelites will
not believe he was chosen by God. God's answer
is that He will provide Moses with a series of signs—
gestures of miraculous power or, some might say,
magic tricks—that will convince the people that
the Lord is with him. In a broader sense, Moses'
question raises the problem that recurs throughout
the remainder of the Pentateuch: how can a people
so scarred by slavery learn to embrace freedom
and its own divine mission?

NOTE: Were you puzzled in the burning bush

episode by God's answer (3:14) to Moses' question of what God's name is?

> And God said unto Moses, I AM THAT I AM: and He said, Thus shalt thou say unto the children of Israel, I AM hath sent me unto you.

The Hebrew for this reply is *Ehyeh-Asher-Ehyeh*, which has also been translated as "I will be what I will be" or "I will be whatever I want to be." Some commentators contend that *Ehyeh* is a variant of Yahweh, making God's answer "I am Ehyeh, whom you know as Yahweh."

Chapters 5–12 depict the efforts of Moses and his brother Aaron, speaking for God, to compel Pharaoh to allow the Israelites to leave Egypt. These efforts begin with a series of contests between Moses and Aaron and Pharaoh's magicians, testing which group can produce the most impressive miracle. At Exodus 7:20 comes the first of the famous ten plagues, blood pollution of the Nile River. Eight more plagues follow in rapid succession, each one more troublesome than the last: frogs, lice, swarms of insects, cattle disease, boils, a devastating hailstorm, locusts, and—building toward the climax— three days of impenetrable darkness.

Were these truly miracles? Or were they a series of natural disasters strung together by later writers as evidences of God's judgment on Egypt? These are questions you must decide for yourself. As you decide, however, you should bear in mind that from the viewpoint of the Bible, the issue is almost irrelevant. Neither the Hebrews nor the Egyptians would have seen such calamities in isolation.

Whatever our opinions might be now, both Egyptians and Hebrews would have agreed that such natural disasters were sure signs that someone's God (or gods) had been mightily offended.

NOTE: Why, instead of this series of afflictions, doesn't God free the Israelites with a single stroke? The answer seems to be that a gradual plan gives God the opportunity more fully to reveal His greatness (11:9):

> And the Lord said unto Moses, Pharaoh shall not hearken unto you; that My wonders may be multiplied in the land of Egypt.

This protracted testing leaves no doubt that the Egyptians deserve their ultimate punishment and allows the Israelites to appreciate the wonder of their deliverance.

At 11:4–5, Moses announces the last and most catastrophic of the ten plagues, the killing of all the firstborn; this judgment recalls the brutality of the murder of the Israelite infants (1:22). Lines 12:1–20 prescribe rituals for the observance of Passover, a festival celebrated by Jews to this day.

Initially, the killing of the firstborn so terrifies the Egyptians that they allow the Israelites to leave. But God having once again "hardened the heart of Pharaoh" (14:8), the Egyptian army, equipped with chariots and horsemen, soon overtakes the Israelites, who have made camp by the edge of the sea. Blaming Moses for their predicament, the terrified Israelites show their willingness to surrender the joys of freedom for the false security of bondage (14:12):

> Is not this the word that we did tell thee in Egypt, saying, Let us alone, that we may serve the Egyptians? [See 5:21.] For it had been better for us to serve the Egyptians, than that we should die in the wilderness.

Moses reassures the people by telling them that the Lord is still with them. In one of the most famous scenes in all world literature (14:21–28), Moses stretches out his hand and the waters divide, allowing the Israelites to escape; but their pursuers get bogged down and the waters close over them, drowning the entire Egyptian army. The Israelites then celebrate their deliverance with a magnificent hymn of thanksgiving (15:20–21):

> And Miriam the prophetess, the sister of Aaron, took a timbrel in her hand; and all the women went out after her with timbrels and with dances.
> And Miriam answered them, Sing ye to the Lord, for He hath triumphed gloriously; the horse and his rider hath he thrown into the sea.

NOTE: You should be aware of some of the historical problems the Book of Exodus raises. At 12:37 the number of Hebrew men taking part in the Exodus is given as 600,000, a number equal to perhaps 20 percent of the total population of Egypt at that time. On the other hand, the only notice taken of the Israelites in Egyptian documents of the period is an inscription reading, "Israel lies desolate; its seed is no more." Is it possible that such a mass movement could have been entirely overlooked by Egyptian historians? Scholars who answer no to that question have attempted to revise the biblical figure down by a factor of 100, to about 6000. But if this revision is correct, what are we to make of the passage early in Exodus (1:7–12) that links the persecution of the Israelites with their rapid population growth?

Freed of the external threat from the Egyptians, the Israelites now face the dangers of fear, doubt, and dissension. The wilderness through which they wander is spiritual as well as physical: the source of their rebelliousness is not only physical hardship but also the lack of a fully developed sense of law, order, and community to replace their clearly defined life in Egypt. For the people's physical needs the Lord provides sweet water, manna, and quail; for their spiritual needs, God will provide at Mount Sinai a new covenant and a code of commandments that will change the face of civilization forever.

Covenant and Commandments
(19:1—40:38)

At Mount Sinai, God commands Moses to tell the children of Israel (19:4–6) as follows:

> Ye have seen what I did unto the Egyptians, and how I bare you on eagles' wings, and brought you unto Myself.
> Now therefore, if ye will obey My voice indeed, and keep My covenant, then ye shall be a peculiar treasure unto Me above all people: for all the earth is Mine:
> And Ye shall be unto Me a kingdom of priests, and an holy nation. . . .

What kind of covenant is this? When you agree to help a friend with her history homework if she'll

THE TEN COMMANDMENTS: THREE DIFFERENT VERSIONS

	Prevailing Jewish	*Roman Catholic and Lutheran*	*Prevailing Protestant and Orthodox Christian*
1	I am the Lord your God, who brought you out of Egypt.	I am the Lord your God. You shall have no other gods before Me. You shall make no idols [graven images].	I am the Lord your God. You shall have no other gods before Me.
2	You shall have no other Gods before Me. You shall make no idols.	You shall not swear falsely [take the name of the Lord in vain].	You shall make no idols.
3	You shall not swear falsely.	Remember the Sabbath day.	You shall not swear falsely.
4	Remember the Sabbath day.	Honor your father and mother.	Remember the Sabbath day.

Prevailing Jewish	Roman Catholic and Lutheran	Prevailing Protestant and Orthodox Christian
5	Honor your father and mother.	You shall not murder [kill].	Honor your father and mother.
6	You shall not murder.	You shall not commit adultery.	You shall not murder.
7	You shall not commit adultery.	You shall not steal.	You shall not commit adultery.
8	You shall not steal.	You shall not bear false witness.	You shall not steal.
9	You shall not bear false witness.	You shall not covet your neighbor's wife.	You shall not bear false witness.
10	You shall not covet your neighbor's house, wife, etc.	You shall not covet your neighbor's house, etc.	You shall not covet your neighbor's house, wife, etc.

help you with your math, the two of you are making a covenant. If several nations agree to a treaty banning nuclear weapons, that too is a covenant— but, like your homework assignment, a covenant between equals. Commentators have long recognized that the biblical agreements between God and the people of Israel do not fit this description. Rather, they are covenants between *unequals*. In that sense they resemble the treaties drawn up by another Near Eastern people, the Hittites, to define the relationship between Hittite rulers and the kings of subject peoples. In such treaties, the sovereign promises to protect his subjects, but only if they follow his laws and remain loyal to him. If the subjects disobey him—if (in terms of the Sinai covenant) they break his commandments—they no longer enjoy the sovereign's protection. The qualities that distinguish the Sinai covenant from such Hittite treaties are, first, that the two parties to it are God and an entire people, the people of Israel; and, second, that the God of all peoples has chosen to make this special agreement with one people only. This is the doctrine of the "chosen people." Such "chosenness" has sometimes been thought to confer on the Israelites some special privilege or source of pride, but it can also be seen as burdening them with an awesome responsibility. The prophets dwell insistently on the terrible punishments awaiting a people that takes such an obligation lightly.

After the Israelites at Sinai have agreed to accept the covenant and have prepared themselves for the giving of the law, God descends to the mountaintop, where Moses joins Him to receive the Ten Commandments, or Decalogue (20:1–17). Like so much else about the Old Testament, the Decalogue

Your Comments, Please.

We are delighted that you have selected BARRON'S BOOK NOTES to assist you in your literature studies. This card is being provided so that you may assist us in our continuing effort to make our Book Notes the finest available. Your comments and suggestions will be sincerely appreciated. Just drop the completed card in the nearest mailbox — the postage is paid.

Thank you for your assistance.

1. **Title of Book Note you read** _____

_____

2. **Were you pleased with the book?** ☐ Yes ☐ No

3. **Was there any aspect of the book you particularly liked?** ____

_____

4. **Particularly disliked?** _____

_____

5. **Would you recommend this book to your friends?**

   ☐ Yes ☐ No   Why? _____

_____

6. **Have you ever used any other book notes?** ☐ Yes ☐ No

   Which one? _____

7. **How would you rate BARRON'S BOOK NOTES as compared to the other series?**   ☐ Much Better ☐ Somewhat Better
      ☐ About the Same ☐ Not as Good

8. **Any suggestions for improvement?** _____

_____

9. **Are there any other titles you would like to see added to the series?** (please list) _____

_____

Name _____

Address _____

City _____ State _____ Zip _____

School name, grad. year _____

_____

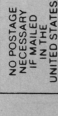

BUSINESS REPLY CARD

FIRST CLASS   PERMIT NO. 14   WOODBURY, NEW YORK

POSTAGE WILL BE PAID BY:

BARRON'S EDUCATIONAL SERIES, INC.

113 Crossways Park Drive

Woodbury, NY 11797

is shrouded in religious controversy. Although there is little doubt about the ethical importance of the Decalogue, different faiths number the Ten Commandments in different ways.

The great code that constitutes most of the remainder of the Pentateuch is of enormous importance for students of religion, ethics, and law. Orthodox Jews regard it as God's supreme self-revelation and gift to humanity. According to Jewish mystics, the Torah existed even before Creation. Most modern scholars, on the other hand, do not regard the Torah as unprecedented. They point out that at least 500 years before the codification of the Torah, the eighteenth-century Babylonian ruler Hammurabi caused to be compiled the famous law code that bears his name. As in the Bible, the law is credited to a divine being—in Hammurabi's case, to the sun-god Shamash. Nor was Hammurabi's code the first. Indeed, from a historical point of view, the Pentateuchal code is only the grand climax to a Near Eastern legal tradition that extends back over 4000 years.

NOTE: The differences between the Pentateuch and its precursors are at least as important as the similarities. Nothing in the Hammurabi Code, for example, quite resembles the monotheism and universalism the Ten Commandments embody. In the Decalogue all the commandments stem from the first—"I am the Lord your God"—and each of the ten is presented as applicable regardless of nationality, wealth, or social status.

From a literary perspective, two episodes in the remaining chapters of Exodus are especially interesting. The first comes in chapter 24, when after Moses tells the people the words of the Lord, the people again answer "with one voice," saying, "All the words which the Lord hath said we will do" (24:3). After the sacrifices and ceremonies that seal the covenant, Moses once again ascends Mount Sinai, and he remains there for forty days and forty nights (compare the Noah story at Genesis 7:4).

In the second interesting episode, Moses is hidden on the cloud-covered mountaintop, and the people—denied not only a visible God but a visible leader—grow restless and confused. They confront Aaron with their demands (32:1):

> Up, make us gods, which shall go before us; for as for this Moses, the man that brought us up out of the land of Egypt, we wot [know] not what is become of him.

In reading 32:2–5, you have a basic choice to make: how do you assess the character of Aaron? How could Aaron not know that in fashioning a "molten" or golden calf he was violating a commandment conveyed explicitly from God through his brother Moses? Do you see him as an unwise or ineffectual leader, yielding to the people's shortsighted demands rather than holding the people to their covenant? Or do you see in his words, "To morrow is a feast to the Lord," an attempt both to postpone the idolatrous ritual and to cast it in the best possible light? How convincing do you find Aaron's explanation to Moses at 32:22–24?

Moses descends from the mountaintop and, furious at the sound and sight of a drunken orgy, smashes the stone tablets of the law. The Lord keeps His word to Moses not to destroy the children of Israel, but He does send a plague to punish the people. As for the stone tablets, God orders Moses to make new ones, which God Himself will inscribe anew. The covenant, though shattered by the faithlessness of the people, will now be restored, as Moses ascends Mount Sinai for another forty days and forty nights. When he returns, the people will know Moses' ever-growing closeness with the Lord by the radiance of his face (34:29–30), as if Moses were the moon and Yahweh the most glorious of the ancient sun-gods.

Leviticus

Overview

Orthodox Jews and fundamentalist Christians agree that Leviticus, the third book of the Pentateuch, was given by God to Moses at Mount Sinai. However, most modern scholars believe that Leviticus was compiled by P, the priestly writer, during the fifth century B.C. It is safer to say "compiled" rather than "composed" because defenders of the documentary theory concede that several parts of Leviticus were written earlier and may be based on ancient oral tradition. One of these older sections is the so-called Holiness Code, chapters 17–26; among its distinctive features is the frequent repetition of variations on the phrase "I am the Lord."

The English title of the book is based on the name Levi, one of the twelve sons of Jacob. You may remember from Genesis 34 that Levi and Simeon avenge the rape of Dinah by massacring the newly circumcised men of Shechem; Jewish tradition regards the subsequent landlessness of the Levites as punishment for this treacherous action.

If you have read the episode of the golden calf (Exodus 32), you may recall that the tribe of Levi is no less zealous in executing God's vengeance at Moses' behest. While the Israelites wander through the wilderness, the Levites are responsible for maintaining the Tabernacle. After the Hebrew conquest of Canaan, the Levites become the Temple priests; they are faithful supporters of the monarchy, upon which their livelihood depends. The association of the Levites with the priesthood underlies the content of Leviticus, for which the title "Priests' Manual" would be equally appropriate. In Hebrew, the title of the book is *Vayikra* ("And He called"), the first word in the Hebrew text.

Themes and Style

Leviticus has undoubted value as a document of social and religious history, especially in relation to the development of the idea of holiness. For some believers, Leviticus also remains a guide to personal conduct. As literature, however, its interest is extremely limited. The narrative thread of Genesis and Exodus is suspended in Leviticus, which is almost entirely legal in content. Prescribed in this book are the laws of ritual sacrifice, other religious observances, the ordination of priests, permitted and forbidden foods, and pure and impure health and sexual practices. Today, only orthodox Jews make an effort to adhere fully to the letter of the law. Even the orthodox recognize that the destruction of the Second Temple, the abolition of the priesthood, and the ending of ritual sacrifice in Judaism mean that many of the commandments of Leviticus cannot be fulfilled— at least not until the Messiah comes and the Temple is restored. Christians, believing that the Messiah has already come, interpret the laws of ritual sacrifice as prefiguring the crucifixion of Jesus. On sexual matters, the influence of the Bible—especially some attitudes toward women and the condemnations of homosexuality at 18:22 and 20:13—is still widely felt.

NOTE: Many people believe that the "Golden Rule" originated with Christianity. In fact, the Golden Rule makes its first recorded appearance in the Old Testament, at Leviticus 19:18: "thou shalt love thy neighbour as thyself." The Golden Rule is cited by Jesus at Matthew 19:19 and repeated elsewhere in the New Testament.

Numbers

Overview

The Book of Numbers derives its title from the census that God commands Moses to make in chapter 1. In many ways, however, the Hebrew title *Bemidbar*, meaning "In the Wilderness," offers a more accurate description of the contents. The book begins about a year after the Exodus from Egypt and then leaps forward to the fortieth year of wandering, when the Israelites are on the verge of entering the Promised Land. Narrative and legislative passages are joined in a way that defies easy analysis.

Numbers is the fourth book of the Pentateuch and, as such, is seen by traditionalists as coming directly from God through Moses. Most biblical critics assign much of the book to P, the priestly writer. The consensus of the critics is that Numbers was compiled after the Babylonian Exile, but that many of its parts are centuries older. Demonstrating exactly which parts come from which period has proved difficult and controversial.

The Covenant and the People

The first ten chapters of Numbers dwell on the census, the special regulations for Levites, the obligations of Nazarites (for more on this topic see the discussion of Samson in the Book of Judges), the construction of the Tabernacle, and various other matters. Finally, at 10:11, the Israelites depart from Sinai. A search party is sent into the land of Canaan, but the majority report is so pessimistic and the response of the people so fainthearted that the Israelites are condemned to another thirty-eight years of wandering. By chapter 21 the narrative has jumped ahead to the fortieth year in the wilderness, and much of the remainder of Numbers describes the beginnings of the long war to conquer the Promised Land.

Let's stop for a moment and think about the extraordinary way that Numbers portrays the children of Israel. Suppose someone asked you to write—or film—the Epic of America. Your task is to show to all Americans, now and in the future, how their ancestors fled oppression in Europe, braved the stormy Atlantic, and crossed the North American continent, subduing and settling the wild frontier. Would you cast these pioneers as faithless cowards and complainers, delayed in conquering the continent not by the danger of the mission but by the anger of their God? Probably not.

And yet that is very much the picture the Bible gives us of the Israelites in the wilderness between

Egypt and Canaan. In chapter 11 the Israelites grumble about their boring diet of manna, demanding the fish and flesh they had in Egypt. In chapter 12, Miriam and Aaron vent their jealousy of Moses; she is punished with leprosy, and Aaron receives a divine rebuke. When most of the search party reports that giants inhabit the land of Canaan, the people are ready to give up their mission (14:1–2, 4):

> And all the congregation lifted up their voice, and cried; and the people wept that night.
> And all the children of Israel murmured against Moses and against Aaron: and the whole congregation said unto them, Would God that we had died in the land of Egypt! or would God we had died in this wilderness! . . .
> And they said one to another, Let us make a captain, and let us return into Egypt.

Two of the scouts, Caleb and Joshua, attempt to reassure the Israelites that if the Lord is with them, they cannot fail—a message the people are in no mood to hear. Again, as in Exodus 32, Yahweh threatens to destroy the children of Israel, and again Moses intercedes. But God can barely contain His anger and disappointment (14:22–23):

> Because all those men which have seen My glory, and My miracles, which I did in Egypt and in the wilderness, and have tempted Me now these ten times, and have not hearkened to My voice;
> Surely they shall not see the land which I sware unto their fathers, neither shall any of them that provoked Me see it:

Thus, except for Caleb and Joshua, an entire generation of Israelites—including all those who came of age in Egyptian bondage—is condemned to die in the wilderness, never having reached the Promised Land.

Why does the Old Testament, the Hebrew scripture, portray the Hebrews in such an unfavorable light? One answer is a reminder that, from the biblical standpoint, not Moses, not Joshua, not Caleb, not any of the Israelites, but God Himself is the hero of the Hebrew Bible. A second answer is that the Bible, always realistic about human nature, insists on showing the scars that slavery left on this particular generation. In short, it portrays the Hebrews as they were, not as (under the covenant) they could be. A third way of looking at the text is as a portrait of ordinary people reacting in ordinary ways to a situation that demands more of them than they are capable of giving. Of course they fall far short of heroism, but do you feel that if you were in their shoes you would do any better? The important thing is that although a generation has been punished, God has left the covenant open—which means that an ideal of human behavior is still within view.

Moses, too, falls short of the divine standard. That is the significance of the episode at the water of Meribah (chapter 20), when because of his moment of anger and disobedience, Moses is forbidden by God to enter the Promised Land. The deaths of Miriam and Aaron are noted in the same chapter. At 27:15–23, Joshua is solemnly appointed as Moses' successor.

NOTE: One striking episode in Numbers deserves special mention: the tale of Balak, Balaam, and the talking ass (chapters 22–24), a folklike story recounted in a mixture of poetry and prose. By this point, the Israelites, taking their roundabout route to the Promised Land, have already conquered the

Amorite king Sihon and are threatening Balak, king of Moab. Alarmed, Balak hires Balaam to put a curse on the invaders. Balak's plan is repeatedly thwarted by the Lord, who converts each curse into a blessing. As for the ass, her speech—which is also the work of the Lord—comes as a poignant plea to Balaam to stop beating her, after their progress is halted by an angel whom Balaam at first cannot see. Commentators have focused not only on the miracle of the animal's speaking but also on the irony that this presumably dull-witted animal sees what the rider cannot.

Deuteronomy

Overview

Deuteronomy is the fifth and final book of the Pentateuch. Tradition assigns this book to Moses' last days, when the Israelites camped in the land of Moab (present-day Jordan) and prepared to enter Canaan. According to Numbers 20:14–21, the Israelites had asked permission of the king of Edom to pass through his territory but had been refused. Thus they were forced to take the roundabout route from Kadesh-barnea southeastward to the Gulf of Aqaba and northward toward Mount Nebo. It is from the summit of Mount Nebo, across the Jordan River from Jericho, that Moses is permitted to view the Promised Land.

The name "Deuteronomy" derives from the Septuagint and means "second law." (The Hebrew title is *Devarim,* meaning "Words," from 1:1, "These be the words which Moses spake. . . .") Organized for the most part as an extended farewell address by Moses, Deuteronomy repeats and amplifies the laws given in the three previous books. A major concern of Deuteronomy not found earlier is the centralization of worship. Although the text does not mention Jerusalem, which did not become the capital of the Israelite kingdom until the reign of David about two centuries later, Deuteronomy does make several references to "the place which the Lord thy God shall choose to place His name in" (16:6) as a site for pilgrimage and worship. Suppression of satellite cults and support for the Temple were key issues while the Kingdom of Judah survived, and most modern commentators attribute Deuteronomy to this period—and particularly to the reign of the seventh-century king Josiah—rather than to the time of Moses.

NOTE: Prominent in Deuteronomy is the theme that if people disobey God's word they will be punished, but if they are obedient they will be rewarded. Watch for this theme as you read not only Deuteronomy but also the histories from Joshua to 2 Kings.

Structure

The first three chapters of Deuteronomy summarize what has happened to the Israelites since the first revelation at Sinai. Moses then goes on to outline the responsibilities the covenant imposes on the people of Israel. Notice how the account of Moses' own failure at Deuteronomy 4:21 differs from that in Numbers 20:7–13. In a second speech, beginning at 5:1, Moses recites the Ten Commandments: among the significant differences between this version and that at Exodus 20 are the mention of deliverance from Egypt and rest for one's workers as reasons for honoring the Sabbath day (5:14–15) and the reversed order of the bans on coveting a neighbor's wife and house (compare Deuteronomy 5:21 with Exodus 20:17). As his second speech draws to a conclusion (chapters 9–10), Moses denounces the faithlessness and rebelliousness of the people and recounts his role in preventing God from destroying them because of the golden calf.

NOTE: Deuteronomy 6:4 brings the central tenet of Judaism, known as the *Shema*. Various translations of the *Shema* have been offered. The King James Version gives "The Lord our God is one Lord"; a modern Jewish translation provides "The Lord is our God, the Lord alone." But what does this line really mean? Does it mean "Yahweh is our God, and Yahweh only"? Or does it mean that Yahweh is unique and indivisible? Does it imply, as the medieval commentator Rashi thought, that "He is 'our God' now, and not yet the God of all nations, but in the future He will be 'the Lord alone' "? All these interpretations may be correct, and you may have another of your own.

For more on the development of Hebrew monotheism, see the section "God in the Old Testament" in this *Barron's Book Notes* volume.

Moses' third and longest farewell speech extends from chapters 12 through 25 and is the final law code in the Torah. Chapters 27 and 28 comprise a long series of blessings and curses, while the next two chapters reemphasize the importance to Israel of loyalty to God and to the covenant. Chapter 31 confirms the passing of the mantle of leadership to Joshua and the transmission of God's law to the Levites, who are to read it in public assembly once every seven years (31:10–13). The predominantly oratorical style of Deuteronomy is interrupted in Chapter 32 by the "Song of Moses," a hymn of praise. Chapter 34 records not only the death of Moses but the passing of an era in Israel's patriarchal history (34:10):

> And there arose not a prophet since in Israel like unto Moses, whom the Lord knew face to face.

The last eight verses of Deuteronomy, which deal with Moses' death and mourning, pose no problem for documentary theorists, who deny that Moses (or God) is in any literal sense the author of the Pentateuch. But these lines do pose a dilemma for traditionalists, who must explain how Moses can have written a description of his own death. Some rabbinical commentators have insisted that God dictated these words to Moses; other attribute them to Joshua or acknowledge the possibility that even later writers made additions to the basic text.

Joshua

Overview

The Book of Joshua is classified as the first of the prophetic books (Nevi'im) in the Hebrew Bible and the first of the historical books in both the Protestant and the Roman Catholic versions. Ancient Jewish tradition credits Joshua with writing his own book, except for a few passages describing his own death and passages of Eleazar, the priestly son of Aaron. Most critics since the nineteenth century have regarded the Book of Joshua as a compilation, like the Pentateuch, from various sources. There is, however, no consensus as to which sources these are or which periods they represent.

In Exodus, Joshua is Moses' faithful attendant, accompanying him up and down Mount Sinai. In Numbers, Joshua and Caleb are the only members of the search party to give a favorable report of Canaan, and thus are the only ones of their generation permitted to enter the Promised Land. The Book of Joshua portrays Moses' successor as both a military leader and a prophet, to whom God speaks directly and through whom God addresses the people of Israel.

NOTE: According to Numbers 13:16, Joshua was born Oshea (or Hosea), son of Nun, of the tribe of Ephraim; he is given the name Jehoshua (or Joshua), meaning "Yahweh is salvation," by Moses. This name change recalls Genesis 17:5–15, where God gives Abram and Sarai the new names Abraham and Sarah, and Genesis 32:28, where the angel with whom Jacob wrestles gives him the new name Israel. Such name changes in the Old Testament indicate an important change in someone's character or destiny.

The Conquest of Canaan
(Joshua 1:1—12:24)
The first half of the Book of Joshua portrays Joshua's commission by Yahweh, the crossing of the

Jordan River, and the rout of the Canaanites by the Israelite invaders. It is now generally thought that the infiltration and settlement of Canaan by the various Israelite tribes took place during the twelfth century B.C. Although the Bible depicts Joshua as a central figure in this campaign of conquest, many modern commentators believe that the historical Joshua played a much more limited role. At 10:36–37, for example, Joshua and the whole people of Israel are credited with capturing Hebron. At Judges 1:10, however, the defeat of Hebron is ascribed to Judah. The conquest of Ai (chapters 7–8 of Joshua) is especially problematical because archaeologists have shown that the fortified city of Ai (which means "ruin") was destroyed in the twenty-fourth century B.C. and was only briefly an Israelite village in the time of Joshua, some 1200 years later.

Surely the best-known section of the Book of Joshua is chapter 6, describing the conquest of Jericho. (For a brief discussion of archaeological problems related to Jericho, see the "Setting" section in The Old Testament Background.) The military tactics employed are extraordinary—indeed, miraculous. Speaking through Joshua, the Lord commands the Israelites, bearing the Ark of the Covenant, to circle the city once each day for six days. On the seventh day, the Israelites, including seven priests blowing seven trumpets of rams' horns, make seven circles round Jericho, shouting for the Lord on the last pass around the city. (If you've forgotten why seven is such a significant number in the Old Testament, review Genesis 2:2–3 and Exodus 20:8–11.) In the words of the famous black spiritual:

Joshua fit the battle of Jericho,
And the walls come tumbling down.

NOTE: Those of you who have seen the fantasy-adventure film *Raiders of the Lost Ark* should be well familiar with the Ark of the Covenant and the magical properties attributed to it. As described in Exodus 25, the ark was an acacia ("shittim") wood chest, decorated with gold, in which the tablets of the law were placed. During the period from Moses to David, the ark was carried from place to place and frequently accompanied the Israelites into battle. After Solomon built the First Temple in Jerusalem, the ark was placed in its innermost sanctuary, the Holy of Holies. Nothing is known of its subsequent history, and it apparently was no longer in the Temple by the time of the Babylonian conquest. The Hebrew term for the ark, *Aron ha-Kodesh*, today signifies the part of the synagogue where the Torah scrolls are kept.

The Tribes and Their Lands
(13:1—24:33)

The second half of the Book of Joshua offers a detailed description of which parts of Canaan the Israelites did and did not subdue, and of the boundaries between the various tribal landholdings. Roughly speaking, the area of Israelite control during the twelfth century B.C. extended a maximum of 30 miles east and 40 miles west of the Jordan River and the Dead Sea. At this time, the Israelites were organized into 12 tribes, or clans, which claimed descent from the sons and grandsons of Jacob. Only the tribe of Manasseh held any land along the Mediterranean coast, which was dominated by the Sidonians (Phoenicians) in the north and the Philistines in the south. In the southeast, Moab and Edom were outside the limits of Israelite control. In addition, several fortified cities remained as Canaanite strongholds, separating the Israelite domains.

There is some confusion as to precisely where, in terms of modern geography, the various tribes settled, but it appears that the northernmost tribes were Dan (after the migration described in Judges 17–18), Asher, Naphtali, Zebulun, and Issachar. Occupying a central position were Manasseh, the largest single landholder, and Ephraim. Farther south were Judah and Simeon (probably absorbed by Judah at an early date), all west of the Jordan and the Dead Sea; and Gad and Reuben, which lay to the east. The Levites, who were landless, received portions of cities from the other tribes (Joshua 21). All these tribes survived as a loose confederation until the establishment of the monarchy late in the eleventh century B.C.

NOTE: Chapters 23 and 24 present Joshua's last words to the Israelites; the farewell addresses of Moses and David, at Deuteronomy 31 and 2 Samuel 23, respectively, are other excellent examples of the form. In the Old Testament, the farewell address, or valedictory, enables the hero to recall the past and survey the future of his people.

The death of Joshua at the age of 110 is recorded at Joshua 24:29. Joshua's death is also mentioned in Judges 1:1. Similarly, the passing of Moses and the succession of Joshua are mentioned both in the last verses of Deuteronomy and the opening chapter of the Book of Joshua. Modern critics believe these apparent transitions reflect the efforts of an editor to turn these separate documents into a continuous historical narrative.

Judges

Overview

When you hear the word *judge*, you probably think of a black-robed figure listening to lawyers argue a case in a courtroom. When you come to read the Book of Judges, however, this image can be very misleading. The biblical judges (known as *shoftim* in Hebrew) were not legal professionals. Instead, these charismatic figures were prophets and warriors. None of the judges ruled over all Israel. But when members of one or more tribes were in peril, these heroes saved them through moral and military leadership.

Rabbinical tradition attributes the whole of Judges to Samuel. Modern critics regard the book as a collection of materials, some of which—notably the Song of Deborah and Barak (chapter 5)—are quite ancient. The bulk of Judges, according to some scholars, was compiled during the seventh and sixth centuries B.C.

Approaches to Judges

Judges not only continues but actually overlaps with Joshua. The slow process of settling in Canaan did not end with that earlier volume, and many of the episodes in Judges—Deborah and Barak against Hazor, Gideon versus the Midianites, Samson and the Philistines—form part of an ongoing history of contact and conflict between the Israelite tribes and neighboring peoples during the twelfth and eleventh centuries B.C. For this reason, whatever its folkloric and legendary qualities, the Book of Judges is a very important historical document.

You can read the entire Book of Judges as the working out of a cyclical view of history. When the people turn away from God, the Lord first sends an enemy to punish them. Then the oppressed people cry out to God, who sends a leader (or prophet) to deliver them. Once rescued, the people pledge their loyalty to the leader and to God, for whom he speaks. But prosperity brings forgetfulness and corruption, and the cycle is repeated all over again.

NOTE: Judges is blunt about the particular sin for which Israel is punished: "they went a whoring after other gods, and bowed themselves unto them" (2:17). Especially seductive were the fertility gods and goddesses of Canaan. From the biblical point of view, worshiping fertility idols was a direct violation of the Ten Commandments, hence of Israel's covenant with Yahweh; the practices of the fertility cults, involving sexual rites with temple prostitutes, were also objectionable on purely moral grounds. Why, then, were the Israelites so easily swayed? Intermarriage with foreign tribes surely played some role, as did simple human weakness. A third answer can be found in the recognition that, as a herding people, the Israelites had no practical experience of settled agriculture until they entered Canaan. In learning agriculture from their neighbors, the children of Israel were also learning the worship of Canaan's fertility gods—to their own God's extreme displeasure.

In probing the historical and moral dimensions of the Book of Judges, you should not lose sight of the fact that this volume has some of the Old Testament's most colorful characters and exciting stories. There is Deborah (chapters 4–5), the only woman among the judges and the only woman portrayed in the Bible as an important military leader. In the same chapters appears Jael, the wife of Heber the Kenite, who resourcefully murders the captain of Hazor after pretending to give him sanctuary. In chapter 6 you meet Gideon, who subdues the Midianites by equipping his army with trumpets, pitchers, and lamps. (The master strategist of this surprise attack is, of course, the Lord.)

Chapter 11 presents the tragedy of Jephthah and his daughter. Jephthah, a mighty warrior, rashly pledges that if God will allow him to defeat the Ammonites, he will offer as a sacrifice "whatsoever cometh forth of the doors" of his house to meet him on his return. When Jephthah arrives home victorious, who should come out to greet him but his only and beloved daughter! You might wish to contrast this story with that of the binding of Isaac. In Genesis 22, the commandment to sacrifice the son was made by God, and hence could be revoked by Him. In the Jephthah story, on the other hand, the vow is made freely—though foolishly—by Jephthah himself, and hence cannot be revoked.

Chapters 13–16 bring the most colorful character of all: Samson. When you read of Samson ripping apart a young lion with his bare hands, binding foxes' tails together with torches, and killing a thousand Philistines with the jawbone of an ass, you may be tempted to see him as a kind of Paul Bunyan or Incredible Hulk. This is an entirely legitimate way of thinking about Samson, who seems to be more brawn than brain. Nevertheless, you should pay close attention to the miraculous circumstances of Samson's conception. Customarily, the vows to serve Yahweh, avoid strong drink, abstain from all unclean things, and never cut one's hair were made by a Nazarite in adulthood, often for a limited period of time. (Regulations for Nazarites, a devout sect, are listed at Numbers 6:1–21.) But Samson, his mother learns from an angel, is to be a "Nazarite unto God from the womb" (13:5). Thus Samson's great strength comes from the Lord, and all his legendary deeds are said to be the Lord's doing. A Freudian sees Delilah's betrayal of Samson as a kind of symbolic castration. Within the context of the Bible, however, the shearing of Samson's seven locks cripples him because it cuts to the heart of his Nazarite power. Renewed growth of his hair (16:22) and renewed faith in God (16:28) are jointly responsible for Samson's fulfillment of his mission, his act of self-sacrifice that brings down the Philistines' temple.

Ruth

Overview

The placement of the Book of Ruth represents a major difference between the Hebrew canon, on the one hand, and the Roman Catholic and Protestant canons, on the other. In the Hebrew Bible, Ruth appears among the Ketuvim, sandwiched between the Song of Songs and Lamentations; the book is classified as one of the five scrolls (Megillot) and is traditionally read on the holiday of Shavuot, a spring harvest festival. Catholic and Protestant Bibles (including the King James Version) make Ruth the third of the historical books, between Judges and 1 Samuel.

The opening verse establishes the time link between Ruth and Judges: "Now it came to pass in the days when the judges ruled. . . ." The historical connection with 1 Samuel, in which David makes his first appearance, is reinforced by Ruth 4:17–22, which traces the descent from Ruth and Boaz to David. Biblical commentators have long recognized that the attempt to provide an ancestry for David was a main purpose for writing the book.

Controversy continues over when the Book of Ruth was written. Certain distinct features of the book's use of Hebrew have been taken as evidence for the influence of Aramaic, hence to a relatively late date of composition—perhaps as recent as 250 B.C. Other scholars, regarding the same expressions as signs of an ancient Northern Hebrew dialect, argue for the ninth century B.C. Still others place the book in the fifth century B.C., after the return from Babylonian Exile; these writers contend that in a period when Ezra and Nehemiah were vehemently preaching against intermarriage, the author of Ruth was making a plea for toleration by pointing out that a non-Jew may be a model for Jews of fidelity to the Lord. The story makes clear that the great King David was the product of the marriage of a Jew and a convert to Judaism.

The Story

In itself, the story of Ruth and Naomi is touching in its simplicity. To escape famine, Elimelech of Bethlehem (in Judah), his wife Naomi, and their two sons migrate to the land of Moab. There the two sons take Moabite wives, Ruth and Orpah. In time, Elimelech and his two sons die, leaving the three women on their own. After the famine ends, Naomi decides to go back to Judah, telling Orpah and Ruth to remain in Moab with their own mothers. Orpah reluctantly agrees, but Ruth insists on going with her mother-in-law (1:16):

> And Ruth said, Intreat me not to leave thee, or to return from following after thee: for whither thou goest, I will go; and where thou lodgest, I will lodge: thy people shall be my people, and thy God my God.

Ruth and Naomi return to Judah, where Ruth gleans—that is, gathers leftover grain—in a field owned by Boaz, a prosperous farmer from the same family as Elimelech. Impressed with the daughter-in-law's devotion to Naomi, Boaz shows Ruth special kindness. Eventually, she marries Boaz, who takes claim to the land left by Elimelech.

NOTE: Gleaning was a way for the poor to support themselves. Every landowner had an obligation at harvesttime not to pick the fields clean but to leave some of the crop for "the poor and stranger" to gather. See, for example, Leviticus 19:9–10.

The story is full of charming details that establish a distance between the time of the telling and the time described; notice especially 4:7, in which

Boaz puts on his kinsman's shoe to seal a bargain. Underlying this custom is the institution of *levirate marriage*, according to which a childless widow was required to marry her late husband's closest kinsman, so that her husband's line could be passed on and his inheritance kept within the family. Since Boaz was not the closest relative, he had to ask his kinsman's permission before he had the legal right to marry Ruth and reclaim Elimelech's estate.

1 and 2 Samuel

Overview

The two books of Samuel and the two books of Kings may originally have been a single four-part narrative, 1–4 Kingdoms. Tradition credits Samuel himself with authorship of those parts of 1 Samuel that describe the events of his own lifetime; this attribution, however, is viewed skeptically by modern scholars. It is now widely assumed that 1 and 2 Samuel and 1 and 2 Kings were compiled in the sixth century B.C., but that the compiler drew on documents as much as 400 years older. According to the critical view, the four books' inconsistent treatment of the idea of kingship reflects the shifting fortunes of the monarchy during the period when the source documents were written. (For a more detailed discussion of attitudes toward kingship, see the section "Points of View" in The Old Testament Background.) It is also possible that the basic history was written at an early date but amplified by later chroniclers with differing viewpoints.

The two books of Samuel treat Israel at a pivotal point in its development. The text of 1 Samuel opens where Judges leaves off, in the middle of the eleventh century. Israel has no centralized state—indeed, virtually no formal government. Agriculture and urban life are still primitive, and at this time the Israelites may not even have had a written language. Less than 100 years elapse between the beginning of the first book and the close of the second, but in that time Israel becomes a monarchy under David, with a new central capital at Jerusalem. To administer such an empire requires a complex system of record keeping, and a new class of literate bureaucrats to maintain it. Almost overnight, it seems, the Israelites transform themselves from a disorganized group of quarrelsome tribes into a powerful empire to which the kings of Edom, Moab, and Ammon pay tribute. For this period of Israelite history, the two books of Samuel are the indispensable source.

Inevitably, discussion of 1 and 2 Samuel focuses on the three personalities who dominate it: Samuel, the last of the judges; the tragically flawed Saul; and David, the shepherd, musician, warrior, rebel, poet, and king. (For more on David as a poet, see the discussion of the Book of Psalms.)

Samuel

Chapter 1 marks Samuel, like Samson, as a Nazarite, dedicated to a life of service to Yahweh. His mother, Hannah, like Sarah and several other Old Testament women, is barren until God intervenes—a sign of the greatness that Samuel will attain. Hannah sends Samuel to live at Shiloh with Eli, an aged priest, and his corrupt sons. One night the Lord appears before Samuel, telling the boy that He will bring judgment on Eli's family because of the wickedness of Eli's two offspring.

NOTE: Chapter 3 begins quite strikingly with the acknowledgment, according to the Revised Standard Version, that "the word of the Lord was rare in those days; there was no frequent vision." This serves to indicate that Samuel, to whom the Lord does speak directly, was rare in his own time. It is also a sign of a change in the way the people of the Bible viewed God's role in history. In the later books of the Bible, Israel's political leaders do not speak with God directly but instead hear the word of the Lord through the prophets. You may already have noticed in the Book of Ruth that although a divine plan is fulfilled—Ruth marries Boaz so that she may bear the line from which David springs—God Himself has no direct part in the action.

After a description of the evils that befall the Philistines when they capture the Ark of the Covenant (chapters 4–7), the text returns to Samuel, who has become a prophet, priest, and judge. By chapter 8, Samuel has grown old and has made his sons judges. But, like Eli, Samuel is not blessed in his children (8:3):

> And his sons walked not in his ways, but turned aside after lucre [money], and took bribes, and perverted judgment.

The aging of Samuel and the corruption of his sons pose a crisis for the tribal leaders, who, fearing anarchy, demand that Samuel choose a king. What Samuel, speaking for God, tells the people is as powerful an indictment of arbitrary power as has ever been written (8:11–18).

Saul

Saul is introduced in 1 Samuel 9:2 as "a choice young man," taller than any of his fellows. Nowhere does the Bible deny that he is a man of virtue and valor, and it is clear from 9:17 that he is God's own choice to govern Israel. Why, then, is Saul such a tragic figure? The immediate cause of Saul's downfall is related in chapter 15. Although Samuel has formally given up the office of judge, he continues to convey to Saul the will of Yahweh. Samuel tells Saul that God wishes him to wipe out the Amalekites completely, "man and woman, infant and suckling, ox and sheep, camel and ass" (15:3). The battle goes splendidly, but instead of annihilating the Amalekites, Saul spares their king, Agag, and the best of their animals—the latter, he tells the furious Samuel, so that his troops could make a sacrifice to the Lord at Gilgal. Samuel, unmoved, curses Saul and kills Agag himself. All that happens to Saul thereafter—his fits of madness, the jealousy that so torments him, his death by his own sword in battle against the Philistines (1 Samuel 31:4)—can be traced to this act of disobedience, which is not Saul's first but is surely his most grievous.

NOTE: The argument between Samuel and Saul contains one of the most powerful pieces of symbolism in the Bible. As Samuel turns away from Saul, the king grabs a corner of the prophet's robe, ripping the fabric. You can imagine Saul standing guiltily, pathetically, a shred of cloth in his hand, as Samuel angrily tells him, "The Lord hath rent [torn] the kingdom of Israel from thee this day" (15:28). The same symbolism underlies the passage in 1 Kings 11 that foreshadows the division of Solomon's kingdom.

David

The Bible introduces David to his royal destiny not once but twice. At 1 Samuel 16:1, in the wake of Samuel's rejection of Saul, the Lord sends the prophet to Jesse of Bethlehem to choose Jesse's son David, a shepherd, as Saul's anointed successor. (Notice that David is the youngest of Jesse's eight sons, consistent with the biblical pattern you have seen earlier in the Ishmael-Isaac and Esau-Jacob stories, among others.) At 1 Samuel 16:17–18, to soothe his fits of depression, Saul sends for David, whom a servant of the king describes as "a mighty valiant man, and a man of war"; note that in 17:39, however, David is portrayed as a novice in warfare. More puzzling still, after David slays Goliath with a slingshot, the text at 17:55–58 gives the unmistakable impression that Saul is meeting David for the first time, even though David has been identified as Saul's armor bearer at 16:21. Most modern commentators are content to explain this apparent contradiction as the product of two distinct traditions that the biblical editor has placed side by side.

The story moves more swiftly and surely from chapter 18 on. Notice the subtlety with which the relationship between Saul and David is presented. Again and again the Bible tells us that the spirit of the Lord has left Saul and lodged with David. But from Saul's increasingly paranoid point of view, David is like a cancer eating away at the royal household. He becomes the best friend of Saul's son Jonathan. He marries Saul's daughter Michal.

His popularity increases with every new military exploit. And when Saul plots to kill David, the younger man can count on Michal, Jonathan, and Samuel, as well as the Spirit of God, to protect him. The increasingly desperate king knows he is fighting a losing battle.

NOTE: You have probably heard the expression "divine right." This phrase embodies the idea that the ruler represents God on earth and derives from God his right to govern. European monarchs could point to God's choice and protection of David as evidence that the Bible gives sanction to the divine right of kings. So powerful is this sanction that even a bad king like Saul enjoys it: David, who has every reason to seek revenge, shrinks in horror from killing Saul because the latter is "God's anointed." But if you look closely at 1 and 2 Samuel, you will see that a monarch keeps his divine right only if he rules in accordance with the will of God as expressed by the law and the prophets. Samuel not only anoints Israel's first king, Saul, but also participates in his overthrow.

Once David leaves the royal household, he is both a fugitive from Saul and the rebel leader of a band of outlaws, gathering up "every one that was in distress, and every one that was in debt, and every one that was discontented" (22:2). As you read the remaining chapters of 1 Samuel, you should pay careful attention to what can only be described as a breathtaking biblical balancing act. On the one hand, David is in open rebellion against Saul and even enters the service of the Philistines. On the

The Empire of David and Solomon

▬▬ Boundary of the empire at its greatest extent

▨ Territory conquered by David

ASSYRIA

ARAM–ZOBAH

PHOENICIA

Sidon

ARAM–DAMASCUS

Damascus

Tyre

DAMASCUS

The Great Sea (Mediterranean Sea)

Hazor

Ashtaroth

Megiddo

Shechem

ISRAEL

Rabbah

Joppa

AMMON

Jerusalem

Ashdod

Jericho

PHILISTIA

Hebron

Gaza

Lachish

Salt Sea

Beer-sheba

JUDAH

MOAB

Kir-hareseth

River of Egypt

Kadesh-barnea

EDOM

Sinai

Ezion-geber

other hand, David never attacks any Israelite set-
tlements, and although he has ample opportunity
to avenge himself on Saul, he is careful to avoid
the moral stain of killing the reigning monarch. In
the end, the king's suicide is the perfect solution
to a delicate dilemma, sparing Saul the ultimate
shame of falling to Israel's uncircumcised enemy,
and sparing David the blood guilt of being responsible for his death.

NOTE: As the Philistines marshal their forces
against him, the desperate Saul disguises himself
(1 Samuel 28), seeks out a witch, and commands
her to summon up the spirit of Samuel, whose
death has been recorded in chapter 25. Notice the
ironies in this En-dor episode. Saul had formerly
banished all "those that have familiar spirits, and
the wizards" on pain of death. Moreover, the angry Samuel not only refuses to help Saul but also
heaps new curses upon him.

The opening chapter of 2 Samuel marks a turning point in the history of Israel. The age of the
judges is over. The death of Saul means that Israel
no longer has two anointed kings but only one—
David. The anointing of David, conducted pri-
vately by Samuel in the first book (16:13), is now
repeated publicly, as David, no longer an untried
youth, returns to Judah in triumph (2 Samuel 2:4).
In the chapters that follow, David consolidates his
reign over all Israel, making Jerusalem his center
of power. To this new capital he brings the Ark of
the Covenant, although his request to build for it

a permanent home, a holy temple, is denied by Yahweh, speaking through the prophet Nathan.

Through a combination of diplomatic skill and military valor, David's kingdom rapidly grows into an empire. But which of David's children will inherit it when he dies? The problem of succession, unprecedented in Israel's history, is complicated by David's sin in arranging the death of Uriah so that David can freely marry Bathsheba, Uriah's wife, who is already pregnant with David's child. As punishment for this gross abuse of power, the child dies within a week of birth (12:18).

But that is only the beginning of David's troubles. Nathan has warned David at 12:10 that "the sword shall never depart from thine house," and the pattern of family misfortunes thus foreshadowed begins in the very next chapter. David's oldest son Amnon—the first in line of succession—rapes his half-sister Tamar, and two years later her brother Absalom has Amnon murdered. Forced to flee the royal household, Absalom organizes a rebellion, proclaims himself king at Hebron, forces David to flee Jerusalem, and takes possession of the royal capital and the royal harem. At a climactic encounter in the forest of Ephraim (chapter 18), the rebellion is crushed, and Absalom—despite David's orders to the contrary—is slain in battle. The Bible heart-rendingly portrays David's inconsolable grief at the news of the death of his son (18:33):

> And the king was much moved, and went up to the chamber over the gate, and wept: and as he went, thus he said, O my son Absalom, my son, my son Absalom! would God I had died for thee, O Absalom, my son, my son!

NOTE: Have you already noticed how fitting it is that David, a rebel against Saul, should be punished by having his own son lead a rebellion against him? You might also recall the family quarrels in some other Old Testament households—those of Adam and Eve, Abraham, Isaac, and Jacob. It is important to remember that in the biblical scheme of things, these are not just family feuds. Isaac and Ishmael, Esau and Jacob, and Jacob's twelve sons are not only brothers but the founders of whole nations and clans.

The quarrel within David's household (which fulfills Nathan's prophecy at 2 Samuel 12:7-12, after David's adulterous affair with Bathsheba) has important political results. Absalom's rebellion reveals and exploits some of the resentments stirred up by the expansion of David's kingship. And, of course, the deaths of Amnon and then Absalom leave open the succession question, which is not decided until the third part of the Book of Kingdoms, which has come down to us as 1 Kings.

1 and 2 Kings

Overview
The dividing point between 2 Samuel and 1 Kings is the death of David and the enthronement of Solomon. In political terms, 1 and 2 Samuel show the rise of the United Kingdom of Israel, while 1 and 2 Kings show its division and consequent decline. The pivotal figure in this reversal of fortunes is Solomon himself, whose reign is portrayed in 1 Kings 1—11:43.

Rabbinical authorities attributed to the prophet Jeremiah the authorship of 1 and 2 Kings, which are placed among the Nevi'im in the Hebrew Bible. In Roman Catholic and Protestant editions, 1 and 2 Kings are the sixth and seventh of the historical books. The prevailing scholarly view is that the two books of Kings were compiled from various sources in the time of King Josiah (whose reign is described in 2 Kings 22:1—23:30), but that additions were made in the middle of the sixth century B.C., after Jerusalem had fallen.

Solomon (1 Kings 1—11:43)

The Solomon of folklore makes his appearance at chapter 3, when, in response to the new king's prayers, the Lord grants him "a wise and an understanding heart" (3:12). Almost immediately, the Bible presents an example of Solomon's fabled wisdom, the judgment between the two prostitutes, each of whom claims to be the mother of the same child. Solomon's solution—to cut the child in two!—appalls the true mother, who declares that keeping half a dead baby is in no way preferable to letting her rival have all of a living child. Hearing her expression of selfless love, Solomon justly awards her the infant. Such insight into human nature profoundly impresses the king's subjects (3:28):

> And they feared the king: for they saw that the wisdom of God was in him, to do judgment.

If Solomon's statecraft had equaled his understanding, Israel might have retained its unity and prosperity far longer. The Bible marvels at the magnificence of the Temple built for Yahweh, at the unparalleled splendor of the royal household, at the spectacular alliance with Sheba (probably Saba, in southwestern Arabia). But as chapters 9 and 11 make clear, all this luxury has its price. Solomon's ambitious building projects depend on forced labor and heavy taxes; when royal revenues fall short, Solomon is forced to sell some northern cities to the king of Tyre. Solomon's marriages to foreigners and importation of foreign craftsmen involve a policy of toleration for foreign cults. Today, living in a land where different faiths flourish in a spirit of mutual respect, you might think of this policy as one more tribute to Solomon's wisdom. But the prophets and pietists among the Israelites didn't think this way at all. They thought that allowing foreign cults to flourish in the Promised Land was the root cause of all Israel's subsequent misfortunes.

NOTE: The literary parallelism between 1 Kings 3:3 ("And Solomon loved the Lord") and 11:1 ("But king Solomon loved many strange [i.e., foreign] women") can be seen as an expression both of the duality of Solomon's character and of the strength and weakness of his reign.

Division and Disintegration (1 Kings 12:1 to 2 Kings 25:30)

Solomon's death at 1 Kings 11:43 caps a reign of more than four decades. Even during Solomon's lifetime, a northerner, Jeroboam, had plotted against him. When Solomon's son and successor Rehoboam refuses to ease the disproportionate financial burdens of the northern tribes, they split off from the southern kingdom (Judah) and choose Jeroboam as their ruler. The remainder of 1 Kings and the whole of 2 Kings trace the history of the Northern Kingdom to the Assyrian conquest, and then the history of Judah to the Babylonian Exile. (For more on this traumatic period in Israelite history, see "The Old Testament and Its Times" in The Old Testament Background.) In the prophetic view that dominates these two volumes, the collapse of both kingdoms represents the failure of the children of Israel, not the failure of Yahweh. Assyria and Babylonia are the instruments of God, employed both to punish an errant people and to clear the way for religious revival.

As you read these books, with their highly judgmental tales of royal ambition and corruption, be on the lookout for certain episodes of particular literary or historic interest. Notice especially the contest of miracles in which Elijah, speaking for God, triumphs over the prophets of Baal (1 Kings 18:17–41); the covetousness of King Ahab and the treachery of the Baal-worshiping Queen Jezebel in the episode of Naboth's vineyard (21:1–29); Elijah's ascent to heaven and the passing of the mantle of prophecy to Elisha (2 Kings 2:1–13); Assyria's triumph over the Northern Kingdom (17:1–6); the era of reform in Judah under King Josiah (chapters 22–23); and the fall of Judah to Nebuchadnezzar (chapters 24–25).

NOTE: The Battle of the Miracles   The Old Testament is not noted for its humor, but the contest (1 Kings 18:1–41) between the zealous Elijah and the false prophets of Baal has a sharp satirical edge. The ninth-century setting is serious enough: God, who has punished the Northern Kingdom for its Baal worship with three years of drought and famine, urges Elijah to meet with Ahab to show the king the folly of his ways. Elijah challenges the 450 prophets of Baal to prepare a bull for ritual sacrifice and then—by prayer alone—to set it afire. Throughout the morning the Baal worshipers chant and leap about, calling on their god. Cry louder, Elijah taunts them; perhaps Baal is talking, or taking a trip, or sleeping. As you read 18:27–29, you should be able to hear the sarcasm in Elijah's voice and see the mingled amusement and disgust on his face as these hundreds of idolaters take even more grotesque but equally ineffective measures to summon the absent Baal. Finally, Elijah, a lone prophet of the Lord, with quiet dignity and calm assurance lays out the sacrificial bull, has the wood beneath it soaked with barrels and barrels of water, and then with a single prayer causes a fire to consume not only the bull and the woodpile but all the stones and water below. Amazed, the people offer their fervent (if temporary) allegiance to the living God and are rewarded with a "great rain" (18:45). As for the 450 unlucky prophets, Elijah has them killed, supremely confident that Baal will not break his stony silence to save them.

1 and 2 Chronicles

Overview

The two volumes of Chronicles hold the eighth and ninth positions among the historical books in the Roman Catholic and Protestant canons, preceding Ezra and Nehemiah. In the Masoretic text, on the other hand, 1 and 2 Chronicles follow Ezra and Nehemiah as the last books of the Ketuvim, and thus as the concluding works of the

Hebrew Bible. This placement reflects the books' late date of composition. Although the events described in Chronicles extend back to the generations of Adam, the text was written while Israel was under Persian rule. The rabbis of the Talmud credited Chronicles to Ezra and Nehemiah; most modern scholars place the date somewhat later, in the fourth century B.C. It is generally believed that 1 and 2 Chronicles were originally one book; probably included in this single volume were the books of Ezra and Nehemiah, which are similar to Chronicles in style and outlook.

Sources and Structure

Little in Chronicles is of literary interest. The author of Chronicles made use of the four books of Kingdoms—that is, 1 and 2 Samuel and 1 and 2 Kings—as well as other documents to retell the history of Israel from Adam to Ezra. The Chronicler, writing from a priestly perspective, is less concerned with political history than with establishing a direct tie between God and the people of Israel, the exclusive legitimacy of David's royal line, and the central role of Temple worship. (The author shows no interest in the Northern Kingdom.) The portrait of David is idealized: he plays a much more important part in the establishment of the First Temple than he does in 2 Samuel, and the embarrassing episodes of Bathsheba and Absalom are not mentioned.

Chapters 1–9 of 1 Chronicles consist mainly of lists—genealogies, census enumerations, the duties of the Levites. The reign of David is described in chapters 11–29. The first nine chapters of 2 Chronicles portray the reign of Solomon, while chapters 10–36 summarize the subsequent history of the Kingdom of Judah, including Jerusalem's fall to Babylon and Babylon's fall to Persia. The mention at 2 Chronicles 36:22–23 of the decree of the Persian king Cyrus is based on the opening chapters of Ezra and will be discussed there.

One famous character who makes his first appearance in the King James Version at 1 Chronicles 21:1 is Satan. At 2 Samuel 24:1, the command to take a census of the Israelites appears to come from God Himself:

> And again the anger of the Lord was kindled against Israel, and He moved David against them to say, Go, number Israel and Judah.

By 2 Samuel 24:10, however, David is convinced that he has done wrong, and that by conducting a census (perhaps for purposes of taxation, forced labor, or a military draft) he has incurred the wrath of the people and of the Lord. The Chronicler must have been troubled by the idea of David's being punished by God for something that God had commanded, so he smooths out the theology by having Satan stand up against Israel and provoke David to conduct the census.

NOTE: The name *Satan* is related to a Hebrew verb meaning "to oppose" or "to obstruct." The term "the satan" appears in the Hebrew Bible most often in the sense of an opponent, a tester of virtue, even a prosecutor in a court of law. (For more on Satan as a tester of virtue, see the discussion of the Book of Job.) The word "devil," in the singular, never appears in the King James or Revised Standard versions of the Old Testament.

Ezra and Nehemiah

Overview

Ezra and Nehemiah, the third and fourth books of the Chronicler's four-volume history of Israel, were probably written during the fourth century B.C. In view of the fact that portions of both books are written in the first person, it is possible that the Chronicler made use of personal memoirs written by (or at least in the time of) Ezra and Nehemiah, but no such documents have survived outside of the Bible. Little in either book is of special literary interest. But the two books are very important sources of information about Israel after the return from exile and about the continuing evolution of the Hebrew faith.

Ezra

The starting point for the Book of Ezra is the remarkable decree by King Cyrus of Persia allowing the Jews of Babylon to return to Jerusalem. But first, here's a little historical background. Having crushed the empire of Assyria and the Kingdom of Judah, the Babylonians were themselves overrun by Persia in 539 B.C. It was the common practice of Near Eastern conquerors not only to loot the lands they defeated but also to take the local gods from their local shrines and bring them to the imperial capital, as a clear sign that the gods of the conquerors were more powerful than those of the conquered. The Persians had a different idea. Within a year after the conquest of Babylon, Cyrus of Persia issued a decree allowing the gods taken captive by the Babylonians to be restored to their shrines, and permitting all peoples—including the Jews—to follow their own religious practices.

NOTE: The place of Cyrus in Hebrew tradition offers an important insight into the Jewish concept of the Messiah. Isaiah 45:1 declares, "Thus saith the Lord to his anointed, to Cyrus. . . . " The word for anointed is *maschiach*, or messiah. This is the only time in either the Old or the New Testament that the title *Messiah* or *anointed* is given to someone not of Jewish birth. (Did you remember that Jesus was Jewish?)

Ezra was a priest and scribe who, during the reign of King Artaxerxes of Persia, headed a band of exiles returning from Babylon. Equipped with broad authority to teach and administer Jewish law to the Jewish community of Jerusalem and its environs, Ezra arrives to find the people's faith diluted by ignorance and intermarriage. He issues an absolute ban on mixed marriages and requires that those who wish to remain within the community must immediately divorce their non-Jewish wives (10:11–17).

The action by Ezra that had the most lasting value is described in chapters 8–10 of the Book of Nehemiah. Ezra gathers the Israelites together and reads to them the Hebrew scriptures, with a running commentary in Aramaic, which by now has become the language of the people. In a renewal of the covenant, the people bind themselves to follow God's laws, and the Torah effectively becomes the written constitution of the Jerusalem community.

Nehemiah

In 445 B.C., Nehemiah, a Jew who holds a high position at the Persian court, hears news from his brother that the Jewish community in Judah is in desperate trouble. Appointed by the Persian king as governor of Judah, he supervises the repair of Jerusalem's fortifications, bans usury (the taking of interest on a debt), and orders that the poor be given back the land and goods that have been unjustly taken from them. Moreover, he is careful to set the best possible example of honesty and frugality in public office (5:14–19). Upon returning to Jerusalem after an absence of a year or two (chapter 13), he campaigns for renewed support of the Levites and the Temple, strict observance of the Sabbath, and (like Ezra) an end to intermarriage.

Esther

Overview

It was with some reluctance that the rabbis admitted the Book of Esther into the Hebrew canon. The form of the story is that of an Oriental romance, the setting is Persian rather than Palestinian, and there is not a single reference to God. Counting heavily in the book's favor was the association of the story with the Jewish festival of Purim, on which the Scroll (Megillah) of Esther was read annually. We are fortunate that some justification was found for its inclusion, for the Book of Esther is a literary gem, a well-told tale of a bigot caught in his own trap.

NOTE: The word *Purim* means "lots," referring to the lots cast by Haman to choose on which date to destroy the Jews (Esther 3:7). The Scroll of Esther is still read in synagogue each year. Each time the name of Haman is mentioned, members of the congregation razz him with noisemakers, for reasons the story makes clear.

Like the books of Ezra and Nehemiah, the tale of Esther takes place at a time when Israel is under Persian rule. The names of certain characters in the story resemble those of the leaders of Persia in the fifth century B.C. Ahasuerus is the Hebrew form of Xerxes, a Persian king who reigned from 486 to 465 B.C.; one of his royal officers was named Marduka, a possible model for Mordecai. However, many plot details square neither with known Persian history nor with Greek accounts of the same period. For these and other reasons, many critics, regarding the story as a distillation of one or more folk traditions, place the date of writing in the third or second century B.C.

As you read the Book of Esther, notice how different it is in style from any of the books of the Pentateuch, the Kingdoms narrative, or the Chronicler's work. God is not appealed to, except indirectly through fasting (chapter 4), nor does He intervene; instead, the story stresses collective action against oppression. Esther has been assimilated into Persian culture and is indistinguishable, except for her great beauty, from the Persian women around her. The narrative is tightly knit, the dialogue is realistic, the portrait of the prideful Haman is psychologically accurate, and the plot reversals are keenly ironic.

The Story

King Ahasuerus, furious at Queen Vashti's refusal to display herself before the guests at a banquet he is giving, holds a beauty contest to find a new

queen. The winner is Esther, who accepts the honor
without telling the king that she is Jewish. Somewhat later, the king elevates one of his courtiers,
Haman, to be chief among his princes, and all the
other members of the court are ordered to bow
down to him. When Esther's cousin Mordecai, who
is known to be Jewish, refuses to do this, Haman
determines to exterminate not just Mordecai but
all the Jews of the kingdom. What Haman does
not know is that Queen Esther is also a Jew and
that Mordecai has already been recorded in the
royal archives as having foiled a plot against the
king's life.

NOTE: Why does Mordecai not bow down to
Haman? The answer is not given in the text itself.
Some commentators explain his action by arguing
that, as a Jew, Mordecai could bow down before
God but not before any mortal. Others, contending that Jews were indeed allowed to show high
civic officials proper reverence, refer to Haman's
Agagite origins (3:1). They point out that the Aga-
gites, or Amalekites, were traditional enemies of
the Israelites, and they claim that Mordecai, in
snubbing Haman, was expressing an ancient tribal
hatred.

After convincing the king that the Jews are a
threat to his kingdom and reinforcing his arguments with a sizable bribe, Haman wins permission to do as he pleases. But Mordecai hears of the
plot and persuades the reluctant Esther (who knows
that to come unbidden to the king is a crime pun-
ishable by death) to help him. The story unfolds

with considerable suspense as, in chapters 5–7;
Haman's plot unravels. After a banquet given by
Esther, the sleepless Ahasuerus learns from the
royal book of records how Mordecai saved him.
The next day the king asks Haman (without nam-
ing Mordecai) how such a hero should be rewarded. When the puffed-up Haman (thinking the
king means *him*) suggests a grand parade, the king
orders that Mordecai be so honored. That night,
at a second banquet, Esther reveals her true origins
and courageously accuses Haman of plotting against
her people. Haman is hanged on the gallows he
had prepared for Mordecai, who takes his place as
the king's chief adviser. By Persian custom, Haman's original decree ordering death to all the Jews
of the kingdom cannot be revoked, but the king
grants the Jews free rein to defend themselves
against attack. The story ends on a nationalistic
note, with the Jews rejoicing at the bloody slaughter of their would-be oppressors.

Job

Overview
Sabean cutthroats kill Job's herdsmen and cattle.
A fire from heaven burns up his shepherds and
sheep. Chaldean raiders slaughter his servants and
camels. A great wind blows down his eldest son's
house, crushing all his children. He is covered with
ugly, oozing, painful sores. His wife mocks him.
And what has Job done to deserve all this?

Nothing, he insists. Nothing at all.

But I didn't do anything. Maybe you've said that
when a parent told you to stop teasing your younger

sister, or when a teacher singled you out for detention, or when a highway patrolman signaled you to pull off the road. Perhaps you noticed the look of skepticism that greeted your repeated denials.

But I didn't do anything. When you see a picture of someone dragged into court and charged with a serious crime, a well-meaning voice inside you may say: He's innocent until proven guilty. But another voice inside you may also say: He must be guilty of *something* or he wouldn't be in such serious trouble.

How do we know who is innocent and who is guilty? What—or who—is the source of undeserved suffering? Is there a logic to life that people can understand? Or must we be content to stand in awe of a heavenly Father who can exalt us or crush us at His own choosing? These are the questions the Book of Job asks. Whether its answers inspire reverence or despair is a question only you can decide.

The Book of Job resembles nothing else that has come down to us from the ancients, although its message bears similarities to Ecclesiastes. Suggested dates for its composition range from the sixth to the third centuries B.C., but there is an archaic feeling to the story that suggests, in the opinion of some critics, a more ancient origin. Other critics, looking at the same evidence, have answered that the Book of Job is the work of a self-conscious and highly skilled writer deliberately seeking to evoke the past.

The Ethical Dilemma
The prologue (chapters 1–2) sets out with brilliant economy the ethical problem of the work. Job, we

are told, is "perfect and upright" (1:1). Recognizing Job's virtues, God mentions him to Satan, who—in his heavenly capacity as a tester of virtue—claims that Job is pious only because he has much to be thankful for. If his comforts are taken away, says Satan, then Job "will curse Thee to Thy face"(1:11). God's permission to Satan to test Job's goodness marks the beginning of Job's sufferings. Later, when the loss of his wealth and children does not cause Job to lose his faith, Satan gains God's permission to afflict his body. This torment Job also bears without cursing God, but he refuses passively to accept his fate without questioning the cause of his afflictions.

NOTE: What does this prologue really accomplish? After you read the prologue, you know something Job and his friends do not know: you know why Job suffers. He suffers because God consents to join Satan in a cosmic bet. What you do not know—what the author never explains—is why God joins Satan in making this bargain.

Ignorant of the drama that has gone on in heaven, the wretched Job and his friends set about the task of puzzling out the Lord's intentions. Chapters 3–37 present an extended philosophical dialogue in which Job's friends suggest various approaches to the problem, and Job finds all of them wanting. When Bildad contends that because God is just, what has happened to Job must be just (chapter 8), Job challenges God not merely to condemn him but to show him the reasons for His anger (10:1–2). When Zophar tells Job that God's ways are beyond human

comprehension (chapter 11), Job, like a prisoner
held on unspecified charges, insists that God at
least make out the case against him (13:22–23). In
effect, Job wants the chance to prove his innocence
to God, in which case God must be guilty of unjustly punishing Job. To Bildad's accusation that
the wicked person is "cast into a net by his own
feet" (18:8), Job demands that his friends recognize
that "God hath overthrown me, and hath com-
passed me with His net" (19:6). The voices of the
friends grow increasingly shrill, and Eliphaz, convinced that Job simply cannot be innocent, begins
to list the sins of which Job might be guilty (22:5–7).
In reply, Job not only denies all his friends' accu-
sations but also imagines other sins that might have
been committed and denies those, too. Round and
round the fruitless dialogue rolls, until the voice
that silences all voices, the voice of God, speaks
from a whirlwind (38:2–7):

> Who is this that darkeneth counsel by words
> without knowledge?
> Gird up now thy loins like a man; for I will
> demand of thee, and answer thou me.
> Where was thou when I laid the foundations
> of the earth? declare, if thou hast understand-
> ing.
> Who hath laid the measures thereof, if thou
> knowest? or who hath stretched the line upon
> it?
> Whereupon are the foundations thereof fas-
> tened? or who laid the corner stone thereof:
> When the morning stars sang together, and
> all the sons of God shouted for joy?

For three chapters the Lord's speech continues,
in some of the Bible's most glorious poetry. Briefly,
what God tells Job is this: When you can create a
world and dominate a universe, then—and only

then—will you have the right to summon Me to account for My actions. A repentant Job embraces this answer and, in the epilogue (42:7–17), sees his friends chastised for their thoughtless and tactless criticism. In compensation for his suffering, he receives double his former wealth and lives out the remainder of his 140 years in peace and happiness.

Job appears to be profoundly moved by God's answer, but are you? Do you feel, as some critics have argued, that God never really addresses Job's challenge? Or do you believe that the Lord's grace in making His divine presence known to Job is the greatest answer and reward He could offer? Are you comforted by the awesome revelation of divine power? Or are you troubled by man's inability to comprehend the purposes for which that power is used? Are you delighted to find that Job does indeed reap his material and spiritual rewards? Or are you disturbed to discover that we cannot know—at least until the voice in the whirlwind speaks to us—who are the innocent and who are the guilty? In short, is Job a work of doubt or a work of faith? The problems are so difficult, the answers so elusive, that a first reading of the Book of Job is only the bare beginning of your journey.

Psalms

Overview

The Book of Psalms is an anthology of 150 poems grouped into five volumes (1–41; 42–72; 73–89; 90–106; 107–150). The unmistakable reference in Psalm 137 to the Babylonian Exile ("By the rivers of Babylon, there we sat down") means that the book cannot have reached its final form until the sixth century B.C. at the earliest. Prevailing opinion during the nineteenth century was that the whole Book of Psalms was a product of the Maccabean period. More recent scholarship has tended to push back the date of composition. Many individual Psalms could have been written as early as the period of the Judges, and there is no reason why David himself cannot have written many of the 73 Psalms that are labeled "A Psalm of David." If you are hazy about some of these dates and periods, go back and look at the time line in the section "The Old Testament and its Times."

The word *Psalm* comes from the Greek *psalmos*, meaning "a song sung to the harp." The Hebrew title is *Tehillim*, or "songs of praise," a phrase that describes many but by no means all of the poems. The entire collection has been called "The Hymn-book of the Second Temple," reflecting the use of the poems for public worship as well as private study.

NOTE: The style and language of the Psalms in English cannot be analyzed apart from the characteristics of a particular translation. To see just how different translations project different moods and meanings, see the comparison based on the Twenty-third Psalm in "Translations and Editions."

Themes

To help you in understanding individual Psalms and in comparing two Psalms or more, the following list shows some of the themes that come up repeatedly throughout the volume. But first a warning: No classification of themes can replace the experience of reading a poem. A single Psalm can move from lamentation to petition to thanksgiving when the prayer is answered. Each of the 150 Psalms repays the closest study—which, to get the full flavor of the poetry, should include reading aloud. If you spend your time memorizing a list rather than reading poems, you are only cheating yourself.

- Hymns of praise to the greatness and glory of God—e.g., 8, 19, 29, 33, 65, 66, 92, 100, 104, 113, 117, 135, 145–150. Included within this group are a number of Psalms that dwell specifically on the role of the Lord as King of the Universe—e.g., 47, 93, 96, 97, 99.
- Hymns of thanksgiving, both individual and communal—e.g., 18, 30, 34, 40, 66, 67, 111, 118, 136, 138.
- Hymns to Jerusalem and Zion—e.g., 46, 48, 76, 84, 87, 122.
- "Royal Psalms" concerned with the qualities, responsibilities, and misfortunes of God's anointed king—e.g., 2, 18, 20, 21, 45, 72, 89, 110, 132, 144.
- Laments usually joined to pleas for God's help. Such laments may be primarily national (44, 60, 74, 79, 80, 83, 89, 94) or personal (3, 6, 7, 9, 10, 13, 17, 22, 25–28, 31, 35, 36, 38, 39, 41, 42, 43, 51, 54–57, 59, 61, 64, 69, 71, 77, 86, 88, 102, 120, 123, 130, 140–143).

Proverbs

Overview

Although the opening verse of Proverbs (*Mishle* in Hebrew) appears to credit King Solomon with authorship of the book, commentators have long recognized that Proverbs is a composite work whose contents were in flux until the dawn of the Christian era. In ancient times, Proverbs probably served as a kind of school textbook, providing materials for study, memorization, and writing practice. Similar collections of wise sayings have been found in Mesopotamia and Egypt, and some of Proverbs appears to have been based on an Egyptian model. Through the King James Version, numerous maxims from the Book of Proverbs have entered the common heritage of the English language:

> He that troubleth his own house shall inherit the wind (11:29).
> A soft answer turneth away wrath (15:1).
> Pride goeth before . . . a fall (16:18).
> A merry heart doeth good like a medicine (17:22).
> A good name is rather to be chosen than great riches (22:1).
> He that trusteth in his own heart is a fool (28:26).
> He that giveth unto the poor shall not lack (28:27).
> Where there is no vision, the people perish (29:18).

Themes and Structure

The first of Proverbs' four main sections, all of which are addressed to a male audience, consists of an extended lecture about the ideal man (1:1—9:18). As you read, try to form a mental picture of this ideal man, what he avoids and what he seeks out. Try also to develop a sense of the personality of the speaker. Is he more likely to be old or young? Rich or poor?

The second section (10:1—22:16), generally thought to be the oldest, consists of a diverse group of sayings, most of which show some kind of parallel structure. Sometimes the parallelism is *syn-*

onymous, with the second line restating and reinforcing the first (19:5):

> A false witness shall not be unpunished,
> and he that speaketh lies shall not escape.

Also common is *synthetic* parallelism, in which the first line states a theme and the second presents an analogy or elaboration (11:16):

> A gracious woman retaineth honour:
> and strong men retain riches.

Often the parallelism is *antithetical*—that is, the second line reinforces the point of the first by stating a contrary example (12:4):

> A virtuous woman is a crown to her husband:
> but she that maketh ashamed is as rottenness
>   in his bones.

The third section (22:17—24:34) is the one most clearly based on an Egyptian model, a collection of sayings attributed to Amenemope, who lived in the eleventh century B.C. Compare, for example, these two comments on money, the first from Amenemope, the second from Proverbs 23:5:

> (1) If riches come to you by theft,
>   They will not stay the night with you. . . .
>   They made themselves wings like geese,
>   And flew away to the sky.

> (2) . . . riches certainly make themselves wings;
>   they fly away as an eagle toward heaven.

The fourth section (25:1—31:31) consists for the most part of additional proverbs of Solomon as recorded in the time of King Hezekiah, who ruled Judah around 700 B.C. This section concludes with a well-known poem of praise for the ideal wife (31:10–31), beginning "Who can find a virtuous woman? for her price is far above rubies." The original form of the poem is an acrostic, each of whose twenty-two lines begins with a different letter of the Hebrew alphabet.

NOTE: The "virtuous woman" poem has been used by social historians to paint a word picture of a well-to-do household in ancient Israel. How does this description of a woman's status and responsibilities accord with the portraits of women given elsewhere in the Old Testament—for example, in Genesis and in the historical books?

Ecclesiastes

Overview

Perhaps you have heard the modern French expression *"Plus ça change, plus c'est la même chose,"* "the more things change, the more they remain the same." This idea, which seems at odds with much else in the Hebrew Bible, is a basic theme of Ecclesiastes (1:9):

> The thing that hath been, it is that which shall be; and that which is done is that which shall be done: and there is no new thing under the sun.

Ecclesiastes announces itself as the wisdom of

the "son of David, king in Jerusalem"—in other words, Solomon—but this traditional attribution is not taken seriously by recent scholars. The late Hebrew (heavily influenced by Aramaic), the Greek-like spirit of individualism and fatalism, the absence of reliance either on the Temple or on religious commandments—all these argue for a date of composition some 700 years after the time of Solomon.

NOTE: The King James Version holds some snares for careless readers. In Ecclesiastes the term *vanity*, so obsessively repeated, does *not* mean excessive pride or self-absorption but rather "worthlessness" or "pointlessness"; the saying "all is vanity" means "nothing has any meaning." The name *Ecclesiastes* itself is rather obscure. In Greek, it means someone who belongs to, convokes, or addresses an assembly or congregation (this same meaning is conveyed by *Kohelet*, the Hebrew title). In modern English, "The Preacher" or even "The Teacher" offers a clearer translation.

Outlook

Do you believe in progress? Do you feel that life is better now than it was a hundred or a thousand years ago? Do you think the world will improve in your lifetime, and do you expect to have a hand in its improvement? Belief in the power of human action runs very strongly through the Old Testament, especially the Pentateuch, but it is important to recognize that not all of life can be controlled by man. That is one way of reading the message of the Book of Job, and the lesson applies equally to Ecclesiastes. So powerful are the underlying cycles of life—the forces of nature, the annual turning of the seasons, the alternating rhythms of day and night, seedtime and harvest, birth and death—that human action barely makes a difference, the Preacher says. Of course, wisdom is better than foolishness, friendship is better than loneliness, obeying the commandments is better than breaking them, and the joys of youth are better than the frailties of age, but we should not delude ourselves into thinking that by living a good life we will necessarily come to a good end or even make the world any better. This is a minority opinion in the Old Testament, but Ecclesiastes' view of life can be found as early as a dark day in Eden (Genesis 3:19): "for dust thou art, and unto dust shalt thou return."

NOTE: Ecclesiastes 3:1–8 is one of the most wonderful pieces of poetry in the Bible. So enduring is the beauty of this passage that a folk-rock arrangement of the lyrics ("Turn, Turn, Turn") became one of the more popular songs of the 1960s.

Song of Solomon

Overview

In the Roman Catholic canon, the Song of Solomon (or Song of Songs) is one of the wisdom books, preceding Wisdom and Sirach, two works regarded as noncanonical in Jewish and Protestant editions. Protestant Bibles classify the Song as the last of the poetic books, while Hebrew texts place it among the Ketuvim, between Job and Ruth (with which it shares its themes of love and springtime).

The title "Song of Songs," found in many Bibles, is a literal translation from the Hebrew *Shir ha-Shirim*. Most modern scholars doubt that the book was actually written by Solomon, although some parts of it may be ancient enough to qualify; as with Ecclesiastes, Aramaic influences on the biblical Hebrew suggest that the book appeared in its final form between 400 and 300 B.C.

Erotic and Spiritual Love

Reading about great love poetry in *Barron's Book Notes* is like trying to savor a gourmet meal by staring at a menu. So, close this book and, if you haven't done so already, read chapter 7 of the Song of Solomon. Then reread it. After that, we'll talk.

If you didn't know it was in the Bible, where would you think this passage came from? A book of Oriental love poems? A romantic comedy by Shakespeare? A 2000-year-old copy of *Playboy*? All joking aside, the distinctive mixture of the exotic and the erotic in the Song of Solomon has posed severe problems for biblical commentators, and few books of the Old Testament have received more varied interpretations.

NOTE: The belief that Solomon wrote Song of Songs, Proverbs, and Ecclesiastes explains why they are described as wisdom literature. One talmudic rabbi said, "When a man is young, he sings songs. When he becomes an adult, he utters practical proverbs. When he becomes old, he speaks of the vanity of things."

A literal interpretation views the Song as an extended celebration of physical love, perhaps intended for use at wedding festivals. But this alone would not have qualified the work for the biblical canon. What did admit the Song to the Bible was a symbolic interpretation that considered the Song's real meaning to be the love felt by God (here cast as Solomon) for His people Israel. When the work was adopted into the Christian canon, this symbolic interpretation was modified to make Solomon a figure of Christ. Thus, Christian commentators see Christ as the Bridegroom, and the Church as His heavenly bride. Other interpreters have viewed the Song as a two-character drama about a country girl who helps Solomon ascend from mere infatuation to a higher kind of love; as a three-character drama in which the king and a young shepherd compete for the young girl's affections; and as an Israelite adaptation of an ancient pagan fertility ritual.

In fashioning your own interpretation of this work, you need not say that the Song is about *either* erotic *or* spiritual love; you might want to say that it is about *both*. The opposition of flesh and spirit is a powerful strain in both Judaism and Christianity, but an equally powerful line of thought in the two religions holds both flesh and spirit to be the dual aspects of a single Creation. In seeking support for an interpretation that combines both erotic and spiritual meanings, you might point to the first chapter of Genesis, in which God creates the physical world, commands all His creatures to "be fruitful, and multiply," and calls everything He has made "very good."

Isaiah

Overview

Until relatively recently, the prevailing view among biblical commentators was that the book of Isaiah was the work of a single prophet, Isaiah the son of Amoz, who lived in Judah during the eighth century B.C. As for the references in the Book of Isaiah to events that cannot possibly have taken place within his own lifetime (for example, the mention of Cyrus of Persia at 45:1), these were credited to Isaiah's prophetic powers. During the last 200 years, the traditional viewpoint has been almost totally abandoned. Chapters 1–39 are now seen as the work of the Isaiah identified in 1:1, but chapters 40–66 are now attributed to an anonymous writer of the postexilic period. To distinguish the two, the name First Isaiah is usually applied to the author of chapters 1–39, and Second Isaiah (or Deutero-Isaiah) to the author of chapters 40–66. Some scholars also distinguish in the latter chapters the imprint of a Third Isaiah.

First Isaiah (chapters 1–39)

While Hosea and Amos are preaching in the Northern Kingdom, Isaiah and Micah prophesy in Judah. The central fact of life for Israel at that time is the expansion of Assyrian power, which topples the Northern Kingdom and comes within a hair's breadth of overrunning Jerusalem. Like the other prophets of his time, Isaiah sees the chariots of

Assyria as God's instruments for punishing the faithlessness of Israel (1:4,7):

> Ah sinful nation, a people laden with iniquity, a seed of evildoers, children that are corrupters: they have forsaken the Lord, they have provoked the Holy One of Israel unto anger. . . .
>
> Your country is desolate, your cities are burned with fire: your land, strangers devour it in your presence, and it is desolate, as overthrown by strangers.

NOTE: The message of Isaiah was political as well as spiritual. As the Assyrian threat grew, Judah was tempted to seek Egypt and Ethiopia as allies. According to Isaiah 20:1–6, the prophet demonstrated against such an alliance by walking naked and barefoot for three years as a sign that the Egyptians and Ethiopians would be conquered and taken naked as slaves by the armies of Assyria.

Isaiah's abiding power lies in his ability to see beyond Israel's present trials. Sounding a theme heard increasingly among the Latter Prophets, Isaiah, speaking for God, forecasts the coming of the "Day of the Lord," a terrifying day of divine judgment (13:10–11):

> For the stars of heaven and the constellations thereof shall not give their light: the sun shall be darkened in his going forth, and the moon shall not cause her light to shine.
>
> And I will punish the world for their evil, and the wicked for their iniquity; and I will cause the arrogancy of the proud to cease, and will lay low the haughtiness of the terrible.

That ghastly prospect is tempered by Isaiah's vision of a messianic age, an era of universal peace that still beckons to us (2:4):

> And they shall beat their swords into plowshares, and their spears into pruninghooks: nation shall not lift up sword against nation, neither shall they learn war any more.

Integral to this belief is the prophecy that a Redeemer will restore Israel's former glory. The passage beginning "For unto us a child is born, unto us a son is given" (9:6) has been taken by Jewish commentators to mean that an earthly king from the royal house of David will restore peace and prosperity in the Promised Land. Christian interpreters see this passage as a prophecy of the coming of Christ, the eternal Prince of Peace.

NOTE: One of the most famous of Isaiah's messianic prophecies appears at 7:14:

> Therefore the Lord Himself shall give you a sign; Behold, a virgin shall conceive, and bear a son, and shall call his name Immanuel.

The "virgin" is understood by Christians to mean the Virgin Mary, and Immanuel—from the Hebrew for "with us is God"—is identified with Jesus.

Second Isaiah (chapters 40–66)
Style and substance shift dramatically at the opening of chapter 40:

Comfort ye, comfort ye my people, saith your God.

Speak ye comfortably to Jerusalem, and cry unto her, that her warfare is accomplished, that her iniquity is pardoned: for she hath received of the Lord's hand double for all her sins.

No longer do we hear the voice of Judah trembling at the onslaught of Assyrian power. Now the Lord has chosen a new instrument—Cyrus, king of Persia—to conquer the enemies of Israel and to allow the Babylonian exiles to return to Jerusalem and rebuild their Temple. But this message of consolation does not apply only to the Jews: Second Isaiah's prophetic vision is one of universal relevance.

Among the many messianic prophecies of Second Isaiah, none was more important in the development of Christian belief than the "suffering servant" passage from 52:13 to 53:12. Who is this suffering servant who "was wounded for our transgressions" and "is brought as a lamb to the slaughter" (53:5,7)? Is he, as a few commentators have suggested, a purely mythological figure, an echo of the "dying god" motif that characterizes so many primitive religions? Is he some historical king of the Davidic line or a martyr in a war against foreign oppression? Is he, perhaps, merely a symbol for the people of Israel itself? All these readings have been proposed by critics who deny the validity of using the New Testament as a tool for interpreting the Old. If, however, you regard much of the Old Testament as a prophecy of the New, and the New as a fulfillment of the Old, then the identity of the suffering servant is clearly Jesus.

Jeremiah

Overview

We are unusually fortunate not only in knowing a great deal about the life of the prophet Jeremiah but also in knowing how his book—or at least a major part of it—came to be written. Chapter 36 relates how Jeremiah summoned a scribe named Baruch to copy Yahweh's revelations to Jeremiah concerning the forthcoming destruction of Jerusalem. The prophet then told Baruch to read the scroll aloud at the Temple. When King Jehoiakim was informed of what Jeremiah had prophesied, he had the scroll cut up and burned, and ordered Jeremiah and Baruch arrested. Undaunted, Jeremiah began dictating a second scroll to Baruch, who not only wrote down everything destroyed by King Jehoiakim but added "unto them many like words" (36:32).

NOTE: The name Jeremiah comes from the Hebrew *yerim-yahu* ("may the Lord exalt"). In literature, a jeremiad—a name derived from Jeremiah—is a prolonged complaint or lament.

In its present form, the Book of Jeremiah reflects the interweaving of several different kinds of materials. Of principal importance are the poems of prophecy (oracles), thought to represent the authentic voice of the historical Jeremiah. Autobiographical prose makes up part of chapters 1–25; biographical prose, much of it by Baruch, contributes to the remaining chapters.

The Life of Jeremiah

Born into a priestly family about the year 650 B.C., Jeremiah begins his career of public prophecy in the thirteenth year of the reign of King Josiah (627 B.C.). The reforms of King Josiah may have silenced Jeremiah for a while, but his prophecies of a coming judgment on Judah resume in 609, with the accession of Josiah's son Jehoiakim. Just as the growth of Assyrian power is the central political fact in the time of Isaiah, so the expansion of Babylonia (which had conquered Assyria) dominates the politics of Jeremiah's time. Like First Isaiah, Jeremiah sees the foreign conqueror as an instrument of Yahweh's wrath—so much so that the prophet opposes all resistance. For if the king of Babylon (whom Jeremiah portrays as the Lord's servant) has been chosen to execute God's judgment, how can the opposition to him succeed (27:8)?

> And it shall come to pass, that the nation and kingdom which will not serve . . . Nebuchadnezzar . . . that nation will I punish, saith the Lord. . . .

Because of such highly unpatriotic—even treasonous—prophecies, Judah's political leaders have him arrested and imprisoned. He remains in custody until the Babylonian conquest (586), after which he finds a final refuge in Egypt.

The Prophetic Mission

What is most remarkable about Jeremiah is not so much the nature of his prophecies but his attitude toward his prophetic mission. Like the Nazarites Samson and Samuel, Jeremiah is called from birth to the service of Yahweh (1:5):

> Before I formed thee in the belly I knew thee;
> and before thou camest forth out of the womb
> I sanctified thee, and I ordained thee a prophet
> unto the nations.

He does not marry nor does he have children, because, he tells us, God has warned him that both parents and children shall die "grievous deaths . . . as dung upon the face of the earth" (16:4).

In reading how Jeremiah's unpopular prophecies—and his denunciations of false prophets—lead to his imprisonment and isolation, you might well have asked yourself: Why doesn't Jeremiah just keep quiet? Why does he keep saying things that so few people want to hear and that get him into so much trouble? Certainly it takes great courage to tell your nation's ruler that he is wrong and the enemy is right. But courage alone is not what drives Jeremiah onward (20:7–9):

> O Lord, Thou hast deceived me, . . . Thou art
> stronger than I, and hast prevailed: I am in derision daily, every one mocketh me. . . .
>   Then I said, I will not make mention of Him,
> nor speak any more in His name. But His word
> was in mine heart as a burning fire shut up in
> my bones, and I was weary with forbearing,
> and I could not stay.

The only thing more painful to Jeremiah than the burden of prophecy is the burden of keeping silent. Try to remember this unhappy, God-obsessed man when you come to read of how another prophet, Jonah, tries to evade his calling.

NOTE: Not all the prophecies of Jeremiah are those of gloom and destruction. At 31:31–34, the prophet offers a vision of a "new covenant with the house of Israel," written in the hearts of the people. This passage, which provided sanction for the belief of the early Christians that they were the bearers of a new covenant with God, is quoted by St. Paul in his Epistle to the Hebrews (8:8–12).

Lamentations

Overview

The Book of Lamentations is called in the Septuagint the Lamentations of Jeremiah, but few scholars today have any confidence that Jeremiah was actually the author. However, it seems likely that the five poems that make up Lamentations were written close to the time when Jerusalem and its First Temple were destroyed by Babylon.

Structure

The first four chapters of Lamentations are acrostics, following a Hebrew alphabetic pattern; the fifth, though not in acrostic form, has twenty-two verses, matching the number of letters in the Hebrew alphabet. The central image of the first poem portrays the whole of Jerusalem as a lonely widow, weeping in the night; line 1:19 implicitly compares the ruined city to a forsaken adulteress (see chapter 2 of Hosea). The second poem offers a more detailed description of the devastation and explicitly casts Yahweh in the role of destroyer. In 3:1–39, the poet meditates on the meaning of suffering. The poet concludes that no calamity can happen unless God wills it, but that the ultimate cause of the suffering is the sufferer's own sins (3:39). Verses 40–47, written in the first person plural, amount to a national confession of guilt, while the concluding verses, which revert to the first person singular, express the hope that the enemies of Israel will likewise be punished. In the fourth poem, the emphasis passes to the individual sufferings of those who were caught up in the Babylonian conquest. The fifth poem, the final lament, gives voice to those who survived the battle and remained amid the ruins.

NOTE: Who is the "I" in chapter 3? Tradition identified the speaker, "the man that hath seen affliction" (3:1), with the prophet Jeremiah. At least one commentator has suggested Zedekiah, the last king of Judah. The chapter can also be seen as an exercise in personification, with the "I" standing for Judah or Jerusalem itself.

Ezekiel

Overview

The prophetic career of Ezekiel (which means "may El strengthen") begins about 593 B.C., four years after Jerusalem has come under the sway of Babylon but seven years before its destruction at the hands of Nebuchadnezzar. Generally speaking, chapters 1–24 prophesy Israel's coming doom, while chapters 25–48, presumably written after 586 B.C., offer consolation to a generation of exiles. Living in Babylon, Ezekiel, who may have been a priest, is a contemporary of Jeremiah, with whom he may have been in contact.

There are many problems with the text, and assessments of which passages are by the "real"

Ezekiel are difficult. Most commentators believe the book was written by Ezekiel and/or his followers during the sixth century B.C., but a few critics place the writing or editing of the book as much as 300 years later.

NOTE: No prophet—not even Moses at the burning bush—receives his calling in more spectacular fashion than Ezekiel, to whom the Glory of the Lord appears enthroned on a flaming chariot (chapter 1). Ezekiel's flamboyant style seems to have made him something of a popular entertainer among the exiles. At least, that is how some commentators read the complaint in Ezekiel 33:32 that the prophet's manner of prophecy has more effect on the crowds than the content of his message.

The Prophet as Visionary

The Book of Ezekiel includes an extended prophecy of the doom of Judah and Jerusalem (chapters 3–24), including in chapter 18 a call to the exiles to repent for their misdeeds and the reassuring message that the innocent will not be punished for the sins of the guilty; predictions concerning the destruction awaiting Phoenicia, Egypt, and the other nations (chapters 25–32); a forecast of Israel's restoration (chapters 34–39); and a code governing the rebuilding of the Temple, the reconstitution of the priesthood, and the redistribution of the land. Amidst this wealth of material, among the most striking passages are Ezekiel's visions of Jerusalem corrupted and then renewed, and of the "valley of the dry bones."

• *The corruption of Jerusalem (8:1—11:25).* Let's

briefly take the part of Ezekiel as he leads his listeners on a visionary tour of Jerusalem, city of
abominations. First the hand of God lifts you by
the hair and carries you from your home in Babylon
to the Holy City. You approach the Temple's outer
courtyard and, finding a weakness in the wall, break
through it to find "every form of creeping things,
and abominable beasts, and all the idols of the house
of Israel" (8:10) being worshiped by seventy elders
of the community. At the gate of the inner courtyard you see women serving the fertility god Tam-
muz, and in the inner court stand twenty-five men
with their backs to the Holy of Holies and their
faces gazing worshipfully toward the sun. Unable
to contain His fury, the Lord lets loose six armed
men to wreak vengeance on Jerusalem, sparing only
the few pious ones, a small saving remnant of the
house of Israel.

A horrifying vision of Judah dominated by foreign cults—but how true is it? No such description
of the profaned Temple can be found in Jeremiah
or Lamentations, and it is difficult to see how
Ezekiel, prophesying in Babylon in 592 B.C., could
be a reliable observer. Was Ezekiel then actually in
Jerusalem, speaking as a ruthlessly honest eye-
witness? Or was he in Babylon, preaching to the
exile community, and exaggerating the truth to
convey to his audience the enormity of the sins for
which Jerusalem had been and would be punished?

NOTE: Paralleling Ezekiel's vision of Jerusalem
destroyed is his vision of Jerusalem restored. At
40:1—43:12, Ezekiel takes his listeners on a prophetic tour of the rebuilt Temple, in the company

of an angle who holds a measuring stick in his hand. The Glory of God, which departed the Temple at 10:18—11:1, returns to His house of worship at 43:5, signifying the full restoration of the Kingdom of Israel.

• *The valley of the dry bones (37:1–14).* Now you are inside the mind of the prophet as the Lord sets you down in a valley that is full of dry bones. Commanded to speak to these long-dead skeletons, you tell them that God will fit them with living flesh. As the skeletons once again become bodies, God orders you to call upon the wind to breathe life into them. You see the spirit of life return to them, as they stand "up upon their feet, an exceeding great army" (37:10).

Lines 11–14 explain that the "dry bones" are the whole house of Israel, which shall rise from the grave through the grace of God and the powers of the prophet. Jewish and Christian scholars have generally interpreted this scene as an allegory of the return of the Israelites from their countries of exile, and not as an allegory of individual resurrection. Belief in the resurrection of the dead did not come to full flower in the Old Testament until centuries later, in the Book of Daniel.

NOTE: Ezekiel's messianic vision, like those of Isaiah and Jeremiah, played an important part in shaping Jewish (and therefore Christian) expectations of a Messiah (37:24):

> And David my servant shall be king over them; and they all shall have one shepherd. . . .

For the influence of the Davidic prophecy on the New Testament, see Luke 1:32 and Romans 1:3. The image of the Messiah as a shepherd appears frequently among the Hebrew prophets and in the Christian scriptures, most startlingly in the Revised Standard Version at Revelation 7:17, "For the Lamb in the midst of the throne will be their shepherd."

Daniel

Overview

The book of Daniel consists of two main sections. The first part (chapters 1–6) tells a series of stories about a character named Daniel who is supposed to have lived in Babylon during the time of exile. The second part (chapters 7–12) recounts, in the first person, four revelations to this selfsame Daniel. Both the rabbinical and the early Christian commentators accepted the stories as historically true and regarded the prophecies as having been written in Babylon in the middle of the sixth century B.C. This view was challenged as early as the third century A.D. by a pagan philosopher, later quoted by Saint Jerome:

> [The Book of Daniel] was composed by someone who lived in Judea in the reign of Antiochus who was surnamed Epiphanes, and he did not predict coming events but narrated past ones. Consequently, what he relates down to Antiochus embodies true history, but if he added any surmises about the future, he just invented them, for he did not know the future.

NOTE: Modern scholars agree that the second part of Daniel does indeed date from the reign of Antiochus Epiphanes (175–164 B.C.), the oppressive king whose attempt to wipe out Judaism sparked the Maccabean rebellion. Even so, the first section may have been written up to 140 years earlier. The portrait of Nebuchadnezzar in the Book of Daniel is regarded by experts in Mesopotamian culture as wholly legendary and without historical value.

Most of Daniel is written either in Aramaic or in Hebrew obviously translated from Aramaic. A chronological listing of the books of the Old Testament that are considered canonical by all faiths would place Daniel last.

The Stories

You may already be familiar with several of the stories in Daniel. In chapters 1 and 2, Daniel and his companions Hananiah, Mishael, and Azariah are brought from Judah to Babylon, educated for the king's service, given Babylonian names (Belteshazzar, Shadrach, Meshach, and Abed-nego, respectively), and, because of Daniel's skill at dream interpretation, promoted to positions of influence in the royal household. (Can you recall another biblical figure who, taken against his will to an alien land, becomes an important royal administrator? If, like the Pharaoh in Exodus 1:8, you "knew not Joseph," you should review Genesis 40:1—41:44.)

Chapter 3 recounts the well-known tale of how Nebuchadnezzar sets up a golden idol and orders all his officials to bow down to it. When the king hears that Shadrach, Meshach, and Abed-nego have not followed his order, he has them cast into a "burning fiery furnace." Miraculously, a fourth figure who looks like "the son of God" (a phrase rendered in a modern Jewish translation as "a divine being") appears in the midst of the flames, and the three Jews step out of the blazing fire with not a hair singed or a thread of clothing blackened.

In chapter 5 we meet Nebuchadnezzar's successor, Belshazzar, who gives a great feast at which a mysterious hand writes a puzzling message on the walls of the palace. The king's wise men are stumped, but Daniel correctly interprets the punning message to mean that Belshazzar will soon be overthrown.

In chapter 6 we are once again in familiar territory. Daniel has become prominent in the government of Darius the Mede. Daniel's rivals, knowing he prays daily to Yahweh, plot to trap Daniel by having Darius issue a decree forbidding anyone for a thirty-day period to address any request to any man or god except Darius himself. Daniel, observed in prayer in violation of the decree, is brought to the king, who is reluctant to punish him but is pressured to do so by the jealous courtiers. Cast into a lions' den, Daniel is saved by God. Not so fortunate are his accusers, who (along with their wives and children) are condemned by Darius and torn apart by the same lions they hoped would make a meal of Daniel.

The Revelations

The last six chapters of Daniel are far more complex than the first six. Through a series of visions, dreams, and revelations, Daniel surveys the history of Israel from Darius to Antiochus and looks ahead to a "time of trouble" (12:1) when the dead will be resurrected, a final judgment will be made, and the mysteries of heaven and earth will be unsealed. This kind of writing is called *apocalyptic*, from a Greek word meaning "to uncover" or "to disclose." The Book of Daniel is the only full-blown example of apocalyptic writing to be found in the Old Testament, but the seeds of this view of the world to come can be found in the idea of the "Day of the Lord," or "Day of Yahweh." This is the day of judgment on which God is to reward the just and punish the wicked.

Originally, the "Day of the Lord" referred to a judgment that took place annually, coinciding with the celebration of the autumnal New Year. Over time, however, the concept was applied to Yahweh's final judgment, a day of terror out of which righteousness would triumph. The Day of the Lord is mentioned prominently by Isaiah, Joel, Amos, Obadiah, Zephaniah, and Malachi, as well as Ezekiel and Zechariah. The idea of the coming Day of the Lord gradually evolved into the apocalyptic belief, evident in Daniel and the Dead Sea Scrolls, that a great struggle was under way between the forces of good (light) and the forces of evil (darkness), and that the forces of good would not triumph until Judgment Day.

NOTE: Of enormous importance in the formulation of Christian theology are the references in both Daniel and Ezekiel to the "son of man," most especially in this messianic passage (Daniel 7:13–14):

I saw in the night visions, and, behold, one
like the Son of man came with the clouds of
heaven, and came to the Ancient of days, and
they brought Him near before Him.

And there was given Him dominion, and
glory, and a kingdom, that all people, nations,
and languages, should serve Him: His dominion is an everlasting dominion, which shall not
pass away, and His kingdom that which shall
not be destroyed.

The Twelve Minor Prophets

Editions of the Old Testament often group twelve
of the prophetic books—Hosea, Joel, Amos, Obadiah, Jonah, Micah, Nahum, Habakkuk, Zephaniah, Haggai, Zechariah, and Malachi. In commentaries on the Masoretic text they are usually called
"The Twelve" or the "Minor Prophets." They are
called minor prophets not because their teachings
are unimportant or unfamiliar (you probably already know some of the Jonah story), but because
all twelve books are quite short. For example, the
whole Book of Obadiah takes only a page or two.

The canon of the Minor Prophets was established sometime between the fourth and second
centuries B.C. A combination of factors determined
the order of books. The Book of Hosea was placed
first because of the phrase "The beginning of the
word of the Lord" (translated in a modern version
as "When the Lord first spoke") in Hosea 1:2. In
general, however, the prophets are given in chronological order as the editors of that time understood it.

Hosea

Hosea prophesied in the Northern Kingdom during the eighth century, before the Assyrian onslaught; he lived at about the same time as Amos, who also prophesied in the north, and Isaiah and Micah, who prophesied to Judah. The text of Hosea has many difficult passages, and scholars believe that some verses dealing with Judah were added by a later scribe.

The book opens with a denunciation by Hosea of his faithless wife Gomer. Whether the account of her faithlessness should be taken literally is almost beside the point. The importance of the story is the parallel Hosea draws between a loving husband and an adulterous wife, on the one hand, and a loving God and an errant people, on the other. Using vivid language rich in similes and metaphors, Hosea, speaking for Yahweh, tells the Israelites that if they continue whoring after false gods, Yahweh will punish them for it. If anyone close to you has gone through a bitter divorce, you should be able to feel in Hosea's words the anguish of Yahweh's having to choose between continued love for His people and the desire to cut Himself off from them completely.

NOTE: Hosea repeatedly calls Israel by the name "Ephraim." Ephraim, the younger of Joseph's two sons, was the ancestor of the Ephraimites, one of the most powerful of the original twelve tribes of Israel. (Joshua and Samuel were both Ephraimites.) The tribe of Ephraim led the revolt that split off the Northern Kingdom of Israel from the Kingdom of Judah.

Joel

The only thing known for certain about the prophet Joel is his name, which in Hebrew means "Yahweh is God." The date of the book cannot be determined; some critics believe the text was written before the Babylonian Exile (586 B.C.) and then rewritten after. The Book of Joel begins with a graphic description of a plague of locusts brought by the Lord as a punishment for the sins of Israel. As is usual in the prophetic literature, the prophet follows with a promise of plenty if the people repent. The book concludes with a more general prophecy of the coming Day of the Lord, on which all the enemies of Israel shall be vanquished (3:19–20):

> Egypt shall be a desolation, and Edom shall be a desolate wilderness, for the violence against the children of Judah, because they have shed innocent blood in their land.
> But Judah shall dwell for ever, and Jerusalem from generation to generation.

The Book of Joel gives you a good chance to see how one prophet comments on another and how the New Testament makes use of the Old. Notice, for example, the way Acts 2 makes use of the apocalyptic verses that begin at Joel 2:28:

> And it shall come to pass . . . that I will pour out my spirit upon all flesh; and your sons and your daughters shall prophesy, your old men shall dream dreams, your young men shall see visions: . . .

Consider also the passage (3:10) in which Joel, describing the coming war for the Lord, completely reverses the prophecy of peace at Isaiah 2:4. Now look at Jesus' instruction to his disciples at Matthew 10:34. To which prophet do the words of Jesus seem closer in spirit? How do you reconcile the apparent differences between the messages of the two prophets?

Amos

Do you know someone who wears all the right clothes, belongs to all the right clubs, seems always to say the right thing at the right time—but who is only out for his own gain, and turns his back on the sufferings of others? If so, you know the kind of person the prophet Amos means when, speaking for God, he says (5:12):

> For I know your manifold transgressions, and your mighty sins: they afflict the just, they take a bribe, and they turn aside the poor in the gate from their right.

Amos prophesied in the Northern Kingdom during the eighth century B.C. The first chapter and part of the second foretell God's vengeance against the enemies of Israel. The major portion of the book, however, warns how God will punish Israel for its immoral behavior, which Amos colorfully characterizes as selling "the righteous for silver, and the poor for a pair of shoes" (2:6). Chapter 7 narrates Amos's quarrel with the priest Amaziah, who intrigues against the prophet by telling King Jeroboam that Amos is plotting against the throne. Chapter 9 concludes with the comforting prophecy that, after a period of captivity and destruction, the people of Israel will be returned to their land and to God's grace. (This chapter is thought by many scholars to be a later addition, perhaps by a compiler who wished to soften the harshness of Amos's earlier words.) Also mentioned in the book are a series of extraordinary natural events—an earthquake, a famine, a locust plague, a solar eclipse—which are taken as signs of divine displeasure.

The Book of Amos is much more important than its size would indicate. Remember that Amos was preaching to the worshipers of Yahweh, people who were convinced that their covenant with God guaranteed their safety. They reacted to Amos's prophecies with hostility or disbelief. And yet, within a few decades, in 721 B.C., the Northern Kingdom was swallowed up by the empire of Assyria, and all its ten tribes vanished from the pages of history. As you read, ask yourself how you would react if a new Amos, preaching a similar message, suddenly appeared in the streets of your town or city. How seriously would you take his warnings? What changes in your own behavior would you make?

NOTE: Nowhere in the Bible is the theme that God values justice and righteousness more than empty sacrifices stated more powerfully than at Amos 5:21–24. After the destruction of the Jerusalem Temple in A.D. 70, lines such as these would encourage the Jews in their attempt to reconstruct their religion on the basis of rabbis, prayers, and synagogues rather then priests, sacrifices, and Temple altars.

Obadiah

The Book of Obadiah is the shortest in the Old Testament, and its origins are among the most obscure. "Obadiah" means "servant of the Lord," suggesting a pseudonym, but it might well have been a proper name. Early Jewish commentators placed Obadiah in the reign of Ahab, who ruled the Northern Kingdom during the ninth century B.C. Later commentators have focused on verses 11–14 as a sign that the book was written after the Babylonian conquest of 586 B.C.

Most of this brief book pronounces judgment on the Edomites, traditional enemies of Israel who seem to have helped the Babylonians sack Jerusalem. The concluding verses dwell on a common prophetic theme: the coming Day of the Lord, when Israel shall be upraised, its enemies cast down, and "the kingdom shall be the Lord's."

Jonah

Probably you remember from your childhood the wonderful story of Jonah and the whale. If you still think that Jonah is a tall tale about a man who lives three days in the belly of a big fish, stop right here and read the Old Testament Book of Jonah—all of it, including chapters 3 and 4.

Now let's review the story—the *whole* story. The Lord calls upon Jonah to go to Nineveh and warn the Ninevites that Yahweh knows of their wickedness. Instead, Jonah tries to shirk his mission and books passage on a ship to Tarshish. Then the Lord sends a great storm, endangering the vessel. All the sailors come out on deck to pray to their deities, but Jonah, still trying to run away from God, hides down below. The shipmaster rouses Jonah from his slumber, and it soon becomes clear that Jonah is the source of the evil that has befallen them. Reluctantly, the sailors take Jonah's advice and throw him into the sea. The storm subsides, and the sailors offer thanks to God for their safety.

If Jonah's secret hope is to fall to the bottom of

the sea and forever vanish from God's presence, he is once again mistaken. The Lord sends a great fish who swallows Jonah, holds him in his belly for three days and three nights, and then (after Jonah prays for deliverance) spits him up on dry land. God again insists that Jonah go to Nineveh, and this time Jonah does as he is told. At Nineveh, Jonah preaches that the kingdom will be destroyed within forty days. Hearing this, the king of Nineveh orders the whole kingdom to repent, so that the Lord may change His mind. And that, much to Jonah's dismay, is exactly what happens. Why, demands Jonah, did he have to go to all this trouble if God was going to forgive Nineveh anyway? The sulking Jonah then moves to the outskirts of the city, where the Lord provides a shady vine to protect him from the broiling sunshine. The cooling shade improves Jonah's mood temporarily, but then God withers the vine until, faint from the heat, Jonah wishes for death. The parable concludes with God telling Jonah that just as the withering of the vine was a bitter loss to the prophet, so to Him the deaths of thousands of Ninevites would have been terribly painful. That is why He was so willing to accept their repentance and spare the city.

Supposed dates for the authorship of the Book of Jonah range from the eighth to the third century B.C. Equally varied are the theories of what the book is really about. You can see in Jonah the figure of the reluctant prophet, unsuccessfully trying (like Moses and Jeremiah) to avoid the terrible responsibility with which God has burdened him. Or you can see the story as a parable about the futility of trying to deny or hide from Yahweh, whom even the storms and sea obey. (Consider what happens in Genesis when Adam and Eve and, later, Cain try to avoid God's judgment.) A very positive approach to the Jonah story is to see it as an attempt to demonstrate God's willingness to show mercy to those who mend their ways. What makes this approach especially poignant is that Jonah, a Hebrew, is rebuked by Yahweh—the God of the Hebrews—for wanting to deny thousands of non-Jews the chance to be saved. The Book of Jonah can thus be seen as a major step in the universalizing of Yahweh as a God of all peoples and in defining the mission of Judaism as concern for all humanity and not merely for one sect or tribe. Considered as a plea for toleration, the Book of Jonah bears comparison with another short biblical tale, the Book of Ruth. For a brief discussion of some of the literary techniques in the Book of Jonah, see the section "Literary Forms, Styles, and Techniques" in The Old Testament Background.

NOTE: In the New Testament, at Matthew 12:40, Jesus foretells His own death and resurrection by saying:

> For as Jonas [Jonah] was three days and three nights in the whale's belly; so shall the Son of man be three days and three nights in the heart of the earth.

Christian interpreters have thus seen Jonah as a Christ-figure, risen from the dead and sent by God to bring salvation to the Gentiles.

Micah

Micah is often linked with Isaiah, and for good reason. Like Isaiah, Micah lived in the eighth century B.C., but he was probably a few decades younger. Both men prophesied in Judah, and both saw the fall of the Northern Kingdom to Assyria as a warning that God's judgment on the south would soon be at hand. There are numerous parallels between the books of Isaiah and Micah; compare, for example, Micah 4:1–3 with Isaiah 2:2–4. This might imply direct influence, or it might mean (taking the critical point of view) that the same sentiments were attributed by an editor at a later date to both prophets.

The Book of Micah opens with a pronouncement of judgment against the northern and southern kingdoms, in part because of the oppression of the poor by the rich. (This theme Micah shares with Amos.) The book closes with a poem of praise to God, who, having punished the guilty, will remember His covenant with the patriarchs and have mercy on those who remain. Between these visions of condemnation and consolation come two remarkable passages. The first is the messianic prophecy that out of Bethlehem "shall He come forth unto Me that is to be ruler in Israel" (5:2)—a passage that has direct bearing on the assertions in the Gospels of Matthew, Luke, and John that Jesus Christ was born in Bethlehem. (That town was likewise the home of the family of David.) The second (6:7–8) is a magnificent restatement of the ethical message earlier delivered by Amos:

> Will the Lord be pleased with thousands of rams, or with ten thousands of rivers of oil? shall I give my firstborn for my transgression, the fruit of my body for the sin of my soul?
>
> He hath shewed thee, O man, what is good; and what doth the Lord require of thee, but to do justly, and to love mercy, and to walk humbly with thy God?

Nahum

Little is known of Nahum, whose name stems from the Hebrew for "Yahweh has comforted." Like the Book of Jonah, the Book of Nahum involves Nineveh, the Assyrian capital. This great city was sacked by the Babylonians and Medes in 612 B.C.; most modern critics assume that Nahum lived around this time.

Chapter 1 consists of a poem in praise of Yahweh. Many scholars regard this poem as a later (and corrupt) addition. The original poem in Hebrew was probably in the form of an acrostic, with each line beginning with a different letter of the Hebrew alphabet. Chapters 2 and 3 retell the fall of Nineveh in stirring martial verse. The prevailing attitude is not, as in Jonah, that all life is precious; instead, Nahum glories in Nineveh's misfortune as Yahweh's judgment on the enemies of Israel. In Jonah, the prophet is rebuked for his lack of sympathy; in Nahum, on the other hand, the prophet feels no mercy, nor does God show any.

NOTE: If, as some commentators believe, Nahum was alive in the year 612 B.C. and was reporting about events he knew firsthand, why is he regarded as a prophet rather than a chronicler? If this question puzzles you, remember that a prophet in the Old Testament sense is not necessarily one who foretells the future but one who speaks for God. There's no doubt from the very first line that Nahum meets this biblical definition. You should know, however, that some commentators have questioned whether Nahum belongs in the exalted company of the other prophets, or even in the canon of the Old Testament. They feel that although the book's poetry is powerful, its outlook is vengeful and mean-spirited.

Habakkuk

In its three short chapters, the Book of Habakkuk meditates on the same question raised by Jeremiah (12:1): "Wherefore doth the way of the wicked prosper? wherefore are all they happy that deal very treacherously?" In all likelihood, Habakkuk lived at about the same time as Jeremiah, when Judah trembled at the expansion of Chaldean (that is, Babylonian) power. A prophet such as Nahum might see the hand of Yahweh behind Babylonia's sack of Nineveh, but how could the Babylonian threat to—and later destruction of—Jerusalem be explained? The usual prophetic answer is that God is using Babylon as an instrument to punish the people of Judah for their wickedness. But why, asks Habakkuk, has God chosen as his instrument a people far worse than the Israelites had ever been (1:13)?

> Thou art of purer eyes than to behold evil, and canst not look on iniquity: wherefore lookest thou upon them that deal treacherously, and holdest thy tongue when the wicked devoureth the man that is more righteous than he?

With Job-like persistence, Habakkuk refuses to relent until Yahweh answers his challenge (2:1):

> I will stand upon my watch, and set me upon the tower, and will watch to see what He will say unto me, and what I shall answer when I am reproved.

God's answer, conveyed to and through Habakkuk, is that Chaldea—greedy, covetous, cruel, and idolatrous—will ultimately receive its judgment.

Until then, all the prophet can do is strive to maintain his faith as the world collapses around him (3:17–18):

> Although the fig tree shall not blossom, neither shall fruit be in the vines; the labour of the olive shall fail, and the fields shall yield no meat; the flock shall be cut off from the fold, and there shall be no herd in the stalls:
> Yet I will rejoice in the Lord, I will joy in the God of my salvation.

Zephaniah

The first verse of the first chapter of the Book of Zephaniah places him in the reign of King Josiah (640–609 B.C.) and identifies the prophet as a descendant of Hezekiah—perhaps the same Hezekiah who was king of Judah around the beginning of the seventh century B.C. Josiah's reign is portrayed in 2 Kings 22–23 as a time of religious revival, and the abuses denounced by Zephaniah are similar to those Josiah sought to stamp out. Those that "worship the host of heaven upon the housetops" (Zephaniah 1:5) are practicing star worship, or astrology; those who "are clothed with strange apparel" (1:8) have slavishly adopted foreign clothes and customs.

Zephaniah—the name means "Yahweh has hidden" or "Yahweh has treasured"—embroiders on themes familiar from other prophets. In a famous passage at 1:14–17, Zephaniah heralds the coming Day of the Lord, already trumpeted by Isaiah and Amos; echoes of Zephaniah's words are found in the medieval hymn *Dies irae* ("Day of Wrath"), which often forms part of the Roman Catholic mass for the dead. The second chapter condemns Judah's neighbors and rivals, and the third opens with a wrathful judgment on Jerusalem as well.

The Book of Zephaniah concludes, however, with a joyous hymn praising the power of God and promising the ultimate deliverance of the children of Israel.

Haggai and Zechariah

The two books of Haggai and Zechariah are generally paired for historical reasons. The two prophets make their appearance in the postexilic period, at a time when Jews have been allowed by the Persians to return to Jerusalem, but the Temple has not yet been rebuilt.

NOTE: For more on this period, see 2 Chronicles 36:22–23 and the books of Ezra and Nehemiah, as well as the appropriate sections of this *Barron's Book Notes* volume.

Haggai. The Book of Haggai (the name means "born on a festival") opens with a portrait of the Jerusalem community in the second year of the reign of King Darius of Persia—that is, in 520 B.C. Those Jews who accepted the Persians' offer to return to Jerusalem have not fared well. The prophet speaks of a scarcity of food, drink, and clothing, which can all be taken as signs of a deeper spiritual unease and of God's displeasure with their enterprise. To the argument that the community is not secure enough to rebuild the Temple, Haggai answers that the community cannot prosper until the house of God is fully restored. Responding to his plea, the community, under the leadership of the governor Zerubbabel and the high priest Joshua, resumes work on the Temple, and within five years the great task is completed (see Ezra 6:15).

Zechariah. Like Haggai, Zechariah—whose name means "whom Yahweh hath remembered"—comes to spur on the people to complete the Temple. But the Book of Zechariah is much longer than that of Haggai, and the message is broader and more compelling. Chapters 1–6 embody a series of eight poetic visions which have as their theme the forthcoming restoration of the Temple and priesthood and, ultimately, the dawning of a messianic age. In chapters 7–8, Zechariah responds to the question of whether the returning exiles should continue to observe the days of fasting connected with the fall of Jerusalem seven decades earlier. His answer is a by now familiar prophetic insistence on righteousness, mercy, and justice rather than ritual.

Most scholars assume that the messianic prophecies in Zechariah 9–14 were uttered by someone else. Opinion is divided as to whether the passages should be traced to the period following the completion of the Second Temple or of the First; most modern writers argue for the later date, after the conquests of Alexander the Great. Zechariah's mingling of messianism with a sense of impending political and religious upheaval was extremely influential at the beginning of the Christian era. In Matthew 21:1–11, Jesus explicitly reenacts the prophecy of Zechariah 9:9:

> Rejoice greatly, O daughter of Zion; shout, O daughter of Jerusalem: behold, thy King cometh unto thee: he is just, and having salvation; lowly, and riding upon an ass, and upon a colt the foal of an ass.

Malachi

Malachi is the last of the Twelve Minor Prophets, and the Book of Malachi marks the conclusion of the Nevi'im in the Masoretic text and of the entire Old Testament according to the Roman Catholic and Protestant canons. Malachi, meaning "My messenger," is probably not a personal name; some early Jewish and Christian commentators held that the true author was Ezra the scribe, but the consensus of modern opinion is that the book is effectively anonymous. (The Hebrew word *malachi* actually appears in 3:1, "Behold, I will send my messenger.") The book probably dates from the fifth century B.C., following the return from Babylon but preceding the reforms of Nehemiah.

Malachi forcefully denounces the abuses of the priests, including the sacrifice of blind, lame, and blemished animals; divorce, especially the divorce of a Jewish wife in order to marry a foreign woman; and nonpayment of taxes, or tithes, to support the worship of Yahweh. The characteristic feature of Malachi's style—the repeated use of questions—appears from the very first verses. The book ends with a prophecy of the Day of the Lord, to be heralded by the coming of the prophet Elijah.

Apocrypha and Pseudepigrapha

Only the briefest mention can be made of the individual books of the Apocrypha and Pseudepigrapha. For a full discussion of what these terms mean and what part they play in the structure of the Old Testament canon, see "The Development of the Canon" in The Old Testament Background.

Among the Protestant Apocrypha, the Book of **Tobit**, classified as a historical book in the Roman Catholic canon, is set in Assyria in the eighth cen-

Books of the Apocrypha and Pseudepigrapha

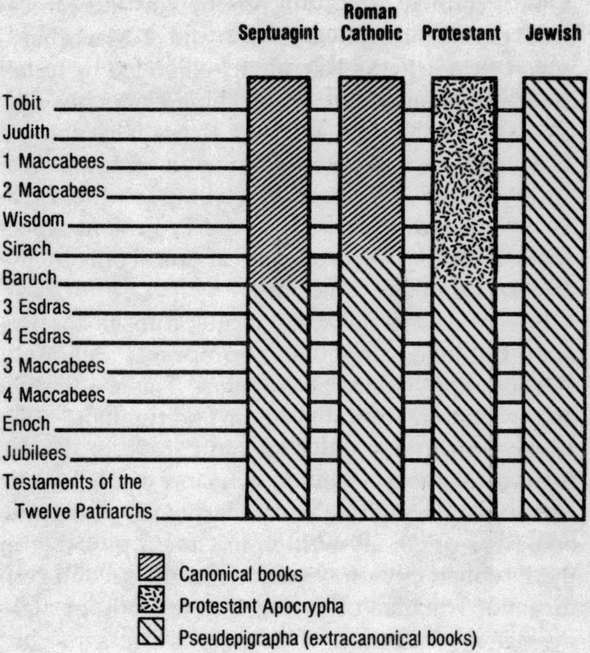
Septuagint
Roman Catholic
Protestant
Jewish
Tobit
Judith
1 Maccabees
2 Maccabees
Wisdom
Sirach
Baruch
3 Esdras
4 Esdras
3 Maccabees
4 Maccabees
Enoch
Jubilees
Testaments of the Twelve Patriarchs
Canonical books
Protestant Apocrypha
Pseudepigrapha (extracanonical books)

tury B.C., although it was surely written much later. It tells the miraculous story of Tobit, a righteous Israelite exiled to Nineveh; of his kinswoman Sarah, destined to marry his son Tobias; and of the angel Raphael, through whose services as a guide for Tobias the blindness of Tobit is cured and Sarah is freed from a demon's curse. **Judith**, also classified among the historical books, recounts the tale of a beautiful young widow who saves her town from siege by charming and then killing the enemy general Holofernes. The book, which mistakenly identifies the Babylonian Nebuchadnezzar as king of the Assyrians, was probably written around the second century B.C. Also products of the Maccabean period are, obviously, **1** and **2 Maccabees**, which chronicle the Israelite rebellion led by Judah Maccabee against the Seleucid king Antiochus Epiphanes—a campaign whose success is celebrated in the Jewish holiday of Chanukah. Another historical book, **3 Esdras**, a retelling of the Ezra-Nehemiah story, appears in the Protestant Apocrypha but is now accepted as canonical only by the Eastern Orthodox Church.

Placed among the wisdom literature in the Roman Catholic canon is, appropriately enough, **Wisdom** or **Wisdom of Solomon**. This meditation on the meaning of true wisdom and righteousness, supposedly written by Solomon, reflects (in the opinion of most scholars) a fusion of Hellenistic and Jewish thought. The scholarly view is that the book was originally written in Greek, probably in the Egyptian city of Alexandria in the second century B.C. The idea of writing a new work (or making a new collection of sayings and poems) but ascribing it to some past worthy was common in the ancient world. Even today, some books still follow this practice: the *Webster's* dictionary on your bookshelf or in your local library has many words the real Noah Webster, who died in 1843, never dreamed of. Another wisdom book, **Sirach** or **Ecclesiasticus**, is a collection of proverbs compiled early in the second century B.C. The basic purpose of the book was to defend the traditional Hebraic outlook against Greek influence. **Baruch**, classified in Catholic Bibles as one of the prophetic books, is attributed to the secretary of the prophet Jeremiah but was probably written much later, in the two centuries preceding the Christian era.

Included in the Protestant Apocrypha are certain additions to other Old Testament books. As you might expect, these additions are incorporated into Catholic Bibles but excluded from Jewish ones. Among the best known of these additions are the passages in the Book of Daniel dealing with Susanna, a virtuous wife unjustly accused of adultery. In this early mystery story, Susanna is proved innocent, and her accusers are executed instead.

Among the many Pseudepigrapha, three books should be mentioned. The Book of **Enoch** is a messianic work that embodies the idea of a preexistent Messiah—that is, a savior whose existence predates the creation of the world and who will preside over the Last Judgment. It is close in spirit to the writings of the Dead Sea Scrolls and marks an important transition from Judaism to Christianity. A second book, **Jubilees**, a retelling of many biblical events, teaches the immortality of the soul and embraces the solar calendar (the traditional Hebrew calendar is based on the phases of the moon.) Finally, the **Testaments of the Twelve Patriarchs**, containing the last words of the twelve sons of Jacob to their descendants, has come down to us as a Jewish work, originally written in Greek, with later Christian additions. Like the books of Enoch and Jubilees, the beliefs contained in the Twelve Patriarchs are similar to those held by the Dead Sea sect and may have helped shape the teachings of Jesus.

A STEP BEYOND

Tests and Answers
TESTS

Test 1

1. The word "testament" is closest in meaning to _____
   A. testimony   B. covenant
   C. tabernacle

2. "The memory of the just is blessed: but the name of the wicked shall rot" is a good example of _____
   A. apocalyptic prophecy
   B. antithetical parallelism
   C. the Deuteronomic view of history

3. The differences between the two versions of Creation in Genesis can be cited as evidence for the _____
   A. influence of Babylonian myths on the Bible
   B. centrality of the covenant
   C. documentary hypothesis

4. Abraham's willingness to kill his son Isaac demonstrates _____
   A. the Hebrew belief in human sacrifice
   B. Abraham's overly impulsive nature
   C. Abraham's absolute trust in God

5. The Golden Rule first appears in _____
   A. the Old Testament
   B. the New Testament
   C. early Greek philosophy

6. The phrase that comes closest to the meaning of "prophet" in the Old Testament is
   A. a spokesman for God
   B. an opponent of the establishment
   C. one who foretells the future

7. The Twelve Minor Prophets are called minor because
   A. their books are short
   B. they all came from Asia Minor
   C. later authorities regarded them as unorthodox

8. Which Jewish holiday is based on the Book of Esther?
   A. Passover   B. Shavuot   C. Purim

9. The prime source of Job's sufferings can be found in
   A. original sin
   B. quarrelsome neighbors
   C. a cosmic bet

10. The description that best fits Jonah is
    A. a seagoing evangelist
    B. a reluctant prophet
    C. the savior of Nineveh

11. Almost every literary form in Western literature can be found in the Hebrew Bible. Discuss.

12. It has been said that God is the only true hero in the Old Testament. Do you agree or disagree?

13. Thomas Henry Huxley called the Scriptures "the greatest instigators of revolt against the worst forms

of clerical and political despotism." What evidence from the Old Testament can you cite to support this view?

14. Show how the Old Testament historical books from Judges to 2 Kings express the Deuteronomic view of history.

15. No one who does not know the Scriptures can fully understand the Jewish calendar. Discuss.

Test 2

1. Which statements about the Septuagint are _____ true?
   I. It was commissioned by Alexander the Great.
   II. It made the Bible available to Jews who knew little Hebrew.
   III. It led to a cross-fertilization of Hebraic and Hellenic culture.
   IV. It influenced the biblical canon for Roman Catholics.
   A. I, III, and IV only
   B. I, II, and III only
   C. II, III, and IV only

2. Why do Muslims regard the Old Testament _____ as sacred?
   A. They consider Esau the founder of the Arab nation.
   B. Muslims honor the Hebrew patriarchs as spokesmen for monotheism.
   C. Muhammad read the Bible aloud in public assemblies.

3. A sign of the Abrahamic covenant is the _____
   A. killing of the firstborn

B. circumcision of male infants
C. rainbow

4. Which one of the following is *not* specifically required by the Ten Commandments?   _____
    A. Honor God through regular worship.
    B. Remember the Sabbath day.
    C. Do not covet.

5. When Moses came down after forty days on Mount Sinai, he found the Israelites   _____
    A. worshiping a golden idol
    B. making sacrifices in honor of his return
    C. preparing to invade the land of Canaan

6. The Book of Ruth shows the blood ties between   _____
    A. Ruth and David
    B. Ruth and Naomi
    C. Naomi and Boaz

7. Which statement best reflects Samuel's attitude toward the Israelites' demand for a king?   _____
    A. In favor, because he wanted one of his own sons to be king.
    B. Opposed, because he thought God was the only king the Israelites needed.
    C. Opposed, because he favored a more democratic system.

8. The first king of Israel was   _____
    A. Samuel   B. Solomon   C. Saul

9. Whom does the Old Testament specifically call *maschiach*, or Messiah?   _____

    I. David
   II. Elijah
  III. Cyrus of Persia
  IV. Jesus of Nazareth
  A. All of the above   B. II and IV only
  C. I and III only

10. The statement "Who can find a virtuous _____
    woman? for her price is far above rubies"
    comes from:
    A. the Book of Proverbs
    B. Ecclesiastes
    C. the Book of Esther

11. Monotheism and polytheism are not just different
    ways of thinking about divine power; they are en-
    tirely different ways of looking at the world. Dis-
    cuss.

12. Assess the reliability of the Pentateuch as a historical
    document.

13. Trace the development of the idea of the covenant
    from Noah to Abraham to Moses.

14. Compare the different ways in which Elijah, Jere-
    miah, and Jonah perceive and fulfill their mission
    as prophets.

15. For Jews, the Old Testament represents the whole
    of the Bible; for Christians, the Old Testament is a
    prelude to the New. Discuss.

ANSWERS

Test 1

1. B	2. B	3. C	4. C	5. A	6. A
7. A	8. C	9. C	10. B		

11. Although much of the Old Testament—not only Genesis but also the books of Samuel, Kings, and Chronicles, among others—consists of chronological narrative, the Hebrew Bible contains a tremendous variety of literary forms. Parts of Exodus, Numbers, and Deuteronomy and all of Leviticus comprise an extended law code. The Book of Proverbs is a collection of sayings, and the Book of Psalms is an anthology of hymns of praise to God. Extended poems include Ecclesiastes, a meditation on the cycles of human life; the Song of Songs, a celebration of love; and Lamentations, a sorrowful remembrance of Jerusalem in ruins. Magnificent poetry is also found in the books of the prophets. The books of Esther and Jonah are as tightly written as a short story, while Job reads like a combination of short novel and extended philosophical dialogue. One biblical figure, Jeremiah, has even given his name to a distinctive literary form—the jeremiad, a prolonged tale of woe.

12. In order to *agree* with the statement, you do not need to argue that the Bible has no human heroes. Certainly there are heroes in the Bible: Abraham the man of faith, Moses the lawgiver, David the poet-king, Solomon the wise, even such prophets as Elijah, Isaiah, Amos, and Jeremiah. The Bible makes clear, however, that these heroes are chosen by God for their heroic mission and remain heroes only to the extent that they express God's will and obey His commands. Especially in the cases of Moses, David, and Solomon, the Bible is not bashful about listing the hero's failings. Angry and frustrated at his faithless followers, Moses disregards the instructions that Yahweh has given him. David sins by committing adultery with Bathsheba and then having her husband killed. Solomon's extravagances oppress the people with heavy taxes and forced labor. One controversial way of *disagreeing* with the statement is to argue that the Old Testament God who banishes Adam and Eve from the Garden of Eden, commands Abraham to sacrifice his son, and makes bets with Satan to condemn Job, a righteous man, to unjustified suffering can hardly qualify as a hero. With a God so arbitrary and unapproachable, the true hero is the one who questions and challenges the divine will. Such heroes are Abraham, when pleading with God to spare Sodom; the prophet Habakkuk, in bravely inquiring why God lets the wicked prosper; and Job, who insists on knowing why he has been so cruelly punished.

13. Those who seek to rebel against tyranny find no shortage of examples in the Bible, including Moses, David, and (in the Roman Catholic canon and the Protestant Apocrypha) Judah Maccabee. Central to the history of the Israelites is their enslavement in and liberation from Egypt, which has served as a model for many freedom movements throughout the centuries. Belief in God and in their own special mission inspired the Jews, both in Old Testament times and after, not to bow down to secular and religious authorities. In the first book of Samuel, the prophet denounces in ringing terms the arbitrary use of kingly power; later, when Saul disobeys God's orders, the prophet anoints a new king. In the second book of Samuel, the prophet Nathan fearlessly holds David to account to a law higher than the king's own. Prophets such as Amos and Micah, speaking for God, scoff at priestly rituals if they are not accompanied by true righteousness and justice.

14. The Deuteronomic view of history is that as long as the people and their leaders follow the word of God they will be rewarded, but if they disobey they will be punished. This theme appears in the Book of Judges as a cyclical pattern. When the people turn away from Yahweh—when they go "whoring after other gods" (Judges

2:17) and worship idols—then the Lord sends an enemy to punish them. This punishment leads the people to cry out to God, who then sends new leaders—in the Book of Judges, such charismatic figures as Deborah, Gideon, and Samson—to deliver them from oppression. With deliverance comes prosperity, but with prosperity comes forgetfulness and renewed corruption, and a repetition of the entire cycle. In the books of Samuel and Kings, the sins of the leaders—the disobedience of Saul, David's adulterous affair with Bathsheba, Solomon's love for foreign women and his tolerance of alien cults—lead to conflict within the royal household and to division in the kingdom.

15. The most important holiday of the Jewish calendar is the weekly Sabbath, in keeping with the fourth of the Ten Commandments and in honor of the seventh day of Creation, on which God rested. The roots of the Passover holiday are in Exodus, when the Lord "passes over" the houses of the Israelites, claiming the firstborn only in the houses of the Egyptians. The Book of Esther is read on and commemorated in the Purim holiday, while the Book of Ruth is closely tied to Shavuot, the springtime harvest holiday. The holiday of Chanukah, while not sanctioned by the Hebrew Bible, has its basis in the Books of the Maccabees, which belong to the Roman Catholic canon and the Protestant Apocrypha. The method of counting years in the Jewish calendar is based on an ancient rabbinical calculation of how long ago (according to the Bible) the world began.

Test 2

1. C   2. B   3. B   4. A   5. A   6. A
7. B   8. C   9. C   10. A

11. On a personal level, polytheism (belief in many gods) placed the individual at the mercy of a variety of contending powers, seen and unseen, not all of which could be placated at any one time. On the other hand, monotheism, as developed in the Old Testament, placed each individual in command of a world that was created for humanity to rule. At the tribal level, belief in many gods afforded no clear sense of the mission or destiny of a people, since different gods could have divergent purposes. In the Old Testament, however, belief in a single God who had offered them His special protection in exchange for their obedience equipped the Hebrews with a powerful way of looking at the world and their mission in it. At a universal level, polytheism implied a world in which rival tribes and their rival gods would exist in a state of perpetual competition. But the developing Old Testament idea of one God and one judgment for all humanity opened the way to the messianic belief in an era of universal peace.

12. The value of the Pentateuch as history is a sensitive and controversial problem. Unquestionably, there are statements in the Five Books of Moses that would be disputed by a great majority of scientists and archaeologists. The statement in Genesis that the world was made in only six days is at odds with the fossil and geological record, which measures in billions and millions of years the age of the earth and the presence of life upon it. The statement in Exodus and elsewhere that over 600,000 adult male Israelites left Egypt is difficult to square with Egyptian documents that mention no such event. Many biblical places, such as Kadesh-barnea, have been located, but many others, including Mount Ararat and Mount Sinai, have not. Various traditionalist answers to this problem include discounting the validity of the scientific and archaeological evidence that conflicts with the Bible, interpreting the text symbolically where the

literal sense clashes with established fact, and expressing the faith that "when all the facts are in" the Bible will prove to be the true Word of God. Most modern biblical commentators accept the findings of scholars in other disciplines and do not seek to treat the Bible as an infallible guide to history and science.

13. The covenant of Noah is a pledge by God never again to destroy the world; no obligations are imposed on Noah or his descendants as a result of it. The sign of the covenant with Noah is the rainbow after a rainstorm. The covenant of Abraham, renewed with Isaac and Jacob, pledges God to make of Abraham and his descendants a great nation, and to give them their own land in Canaan. In general, the obligations imposed on Abraham and his posterity are faith in and obedience to Yahweh. The sign of this covenant—the circumcision of male infants—is also the first specific requirement imposed on the people of Israel. The covenant of Moses, acknowledged by the people of Israel at Mount Sinai, binds God to preserve the people of Israel as long as they agree to receive the divine commandments, live by them, and teach them to their children. The signs of this covenant are the tablets of the law.

14. The fundamental mission of a prophet is to act as a spokesman for God. Elijah, who prophesies in the ninth century B.C., is moved by an irrepressible zeal for the Lord. In a time when Israel's political leaders seek accommodation with the nation's pagan neighbors, he exposes the prophets of the fertility cults as frauds and proves Yahweh to be the real miracle worker. Jeremiah also is steadfast for the Lord, but for his prophecies of destruction, uttered in the late seventh and early sixth centuries B.C., the civil authorities have him flogged, tried for blasphemy, and thrown into prison. He views the task of prophecy as a painful burden he cannot give up. Jonah, who prophesies after the Babylonian Exile, regards the calling of the Lord as such a chore that he tries to shirk it. He ultimately fulfills his prophetic task not by zeal or strength of will but because the Lord will not let him escape his mission.

15. Taken literally, the statement is true, since no "complete" Jewish edition of the Bible includes the Christian Scriptures, while every "complete" Christian edition of the Bible starts with the Old Testament and ends with the New. You might want to point out, however, that the statement applies mainly to matters of religious belief; for purposes of scholarship and literary understanding, Christians can and do attempt to study the Old Testament on its own terms, in the context of ancient Israelite culture, just as Jews seek to understand the New Testament in its historical context. The rabbis who definitively established the Hebrew canon after the destruction of the Second Temple in A.D. 70 were influenced by the belief that divine inspiration had stopped after Ezra, in the fifth century B.C. The early Christians, on the other hand, saw the advent of Jesus five centuries later as God's most profound revelation to humanity. They did not reject the Hebrew Scriptures, with which many of them were well familiar; instead, they sought to reinterpret the ancient texts in the light of their own religious experiences. This difference in outlook is most evident in the treatment of the Old Testament passages prophesying the coming of a Messiah. Jewish authorities after the time of Jesus continued to view such prophecies as a promise of a great age that had not yet arrived, while Christian commentators interpreted many such texts as having been fulfilled by the coming of Christ Jesus.

Term Paper Ideas and other Topics for Writing

Characters

Compare and contrast the following pairs of characters, considering not only their personality traits but also the role each character plays in the Old Testament narrative.

1. Jacob and Esau

2. Moses and Aaron

3. Samuel and Saul

4. David and Solomon

Analysis and Interpretation

Each of the following has been the subject of much critical controversy. Summarize the conflicting views on each topic and then offer your own interpretation, based on a careful analysis of the biblical text.

1. How "fortunate" was the fall of Adam and Eve?

2. God, Abraham, and the binding of Isaac

3. David as a rebel

4. Solomon's reign—triumph or disaster?

5. The character of God in the Book of Job

6. Women and men of the Bible—a feminist interpretation

Old Testament Concepts

Analyze in detail the meaning and development in the Old Testament of a concept central to Hebrew belief.

1. Monotheism

2. Covenants and the meaning of "chosenness"

3. Messianism

4. Sacrifices, priesthood, and the Temple

5. The role of the prophet

Old Testament Influences

Trace the influence of the Old Testament on subsequent developments in religion and the arts.

1. The Old Testament and the New

2. Hebrew belief and the teachings of Muhammad

3. The Hebrew Bible and the Protestant Reformation

4. The King James Version and English literature

5. Old Testament characters in art and/or music

The Old Testament Today

Assess the impact of the Old Testament on contemporary life and thought.

1. The Book of Genesis and modern science

2. Zionism and the Old Testament

3. The documentary hypothesis and its critics

4. Archaeology and the Bible

5. Implications of the Dead Sea Scrolls

Further Reading
EDITIONS OF THE BIBLE

The Anchor Bible. Garden City, N.Y.: Doubleday, 1964–. A modern multivolume scholarly translation still under way.

The Holy Bible. New York: P. J. Kenedy, 1961. Includes the Old Testament in the Douay (Catholic) version of 1609.

The Holy Bible, Containing the Old and New Testaments: Authorized King James Version. Edited by Rev. C. I. Scofield, D.D. New York: Oxford University Press, 1945. Includes commentary, cross-references, and traditional chronology.

The Interpreter's Bible. Vols. 1–6. Nashville: Abingdon Press, 1952–56. The King James and Revised Standard versions side by side with detailed commentary.

The Jerusalem Bible. Garden City, N.Y.: Doubleday, 1966. A modern Dominican Catholic translation.

The Torah: The Five Books of Moses. The Prophets: Nevi'im. The Writings: Kethubim. 3 vols. Philadelphia: Jewish Publication Society of America, 1962–82. A modern translation of the traditional Hebrew text.

REFERENCE WORKS

Aharoni, Yohanan, and Michael Avi-Yonah. *The Macmillan Bible Atlas.* New York: Macmillan, 1968. Clear and authoritative maps and texts keyed to passages of the Old and New Testaments.

Encyclopaedia Judaica. 16 vols. Jerusalem: Keter, 1972. Up-to-date scholarship from a Jewish point of view.

The Interpreter's Dictionary of the Bible. 4 vols. with supp. Nashville: Abingdon, 1962–76. Short scholarly articles on important Old and New Testament topics.

McKenzie, John L., S.J. *Dictionary of the Bible.* New York:

Macmillan, 1965. A handy illustrated one-volume guide to some 2000 biblical topics.

The New Catholic Encyclopedia. 15 vols. New York: McGraw-Hill, 1967. Numerous biblical topics viewed from the standpoints of Catholic theology and modern scholarship.

Woods, Ralph L., ed. *The World Treasury of Religious Quotations.* New York: Hawthorn, 1966. A well-indexed compendium of short quotations from diverse sources.

SECONDARY WORKS AND RELATED MATERIALS

Alter, Robert. *The Art of Biblical Narrative.* New York: Basic Books, 1981. Sensitive analysis of Old Testament themes and narrative techniques.

Bright, John. *A History of Israel.* Philadelphia: Westminster Press, 1981. Well-documented history of the people of Israel as revealed in the Old Testament and other historical records.

Everyday Life in Bible Times. Washington, D.C.: National Geographic Society, 1967. Beautifully illustrated guide to the social history of the biblical period.

Frye, Northrop. *The Great Code: The Bible and Literature.* New York: Harcourt Brace Jovanovich, 1982. Complex investigation of biblical archetypes and metaphors and their impact on the Western creative imagination.

Kierkegaard, Søren. *Fear and Trembling and the Sickness unto Death.* Princeton, N.J.: Princeton University Press, 1968. The nineteenth-century Danish philosopher's troubling commentary on the Abraham-Isaac story.

Pritchard, James B., ed. *Ancient Near Eastern Texts Relating to the Old Testament.* 3rd ed. with supp. Princeton, N.J.: Princeton University Press, 1969. Historical documents from the Near Eastern and Egyptian traditions.

Rashi's Commentaries on the Pentateuch. Edited by Chaim Pearl. New York: Norton, 1970. Rashi, a popular Jewish commentator, has also influenced Christian scholars.

Sandmel, Samuel. *The Hebrew Scriptures: An Introduction to Their Literature and Religious Ideas.* New York: Knopf, 1963. Old Testament interpretation by a distinguished rabbi and educator.

Thompson, Leonard L. *Introducing Biblical Literature: A More Fantastic Country.* Englewood Cliffs, N.J.: Prentice-Hall, 1978. Sensitive discussion of biblical language and symbolism.

Trible, Phyllis. *God and the Rhetoric of Sexuality.* Philadelphia: Fortress Press, 1978. Analysis of Old Testament texts from a feminist perspective.

The Commentators

No work of Western literature has appeared in more editions or evoked more comment than the Bible. Not only have a vast number of books been written about the Bible, but virtually every important thinker in the Western tradition has left some comment about the Bible and its impact on his or her life and thought. The following quotations are only the barest sampling of comments on the Old Testament. Some of them may surprise, even shock you. All are intended to open the discussion for you, not to end it.

Ancient

Why was the Torah not given in the land of Israel? In order that the nations of the world should not have an excuse and say: "Because it was given in Israel's land, therefore we did not accept it."

—From the *Midrash* (*Jewish traditions*)

Think not that I am come to destroy the law, or the prophets: I am not come to destroy, but to fulfill.

For verily I say unto you, Till heaven and earth pass, one jot or one tittle shall in no wise pass from the law, till all be fulfilled.

Whosoever therefore shall break one of these least commandments, and shall teach men so, he shall be called the least in the kingdom of heaven: but whosoever shall do and teach them, the same shall be called great in the kingdom of heaven.

> —*From* The Gospel According to
> St. Matthew 5:17–19, *quoted from
> the King James Version*

Christ has obtained a ministry which is as much more excellent than the old as the covenant he mediates is better, since it is enacted on better promises. For if that first covenant [with Abraham and his descendants] had been faultless, there would have been no occasion for a second. . . .

In speaking of a new covenant he [Christ] treats the first as obsolete. And what is becoming obsolete and growing old is ready to vanish away.

> —*From* The Letter to the Hebrews
> 8:6–7, 13, *quoted from the Revised
> Standard Version*

Whatever they can really demonstrate to be true of physical nature we must show to be capable of reconciliation with our Scriptures; and whatever they assert in their treatises which is contrary to these Scriptures of ours, that is to the Catholic faith, we must either prove it as well as we can to be entirely false, or at all events we must, without the smallest hesitation, believe it to be so.

> —*St. Augustine, from* De Genesi ad
> litteratum, 415

Why . . . did the Torah begin with the account of the Creation? In order to illustrate that God the Creator owns the whole world. So, if the peoples of the world shall say to Israel: "You are robbers in conquering the territory of the seven Canaanite nations," Israel can answer them: "All the earth belongs to God—he created it, so He can give it to whomsoever He wills. When He wished He gave it to them, then when He wished He took it from them and gave it to us."

> —From Rashi's commentary on
> Genesis 1:1, *11th century*

Every Israelite is under an obligation to study Torah, whether he is poor or rich, in sound health or ailing, in the vigor of youth or very old and feeble. Even a man so poor that he is maintained by charity or goes begging from door to door, as also a man with a wife and children to support, is under the obligation to set aside a definite period during the day and at night for the study of the Torah. . . .

> —*Maimonides, from the* Mishneh
> Torah 1:8, *1170–1180*

Modern

The English Bible is a book which, if everything else in our language should perish, would alone suffice to show the whole extent of its purity and power.

> —*Thomas Babington Macaulay, from
> the* Edinburgh Review, *1828*

I had gradually come, by this time, to see that the Old Testament from its manifestly false history of the world and from its attributing to God the feelings of a revengeful tyrant, was no more to be trusted than the sacred books of the Hindoos, or the beliefs of any barbarian.

> —*Charles Darwin (1809–82), from
> his posthumously published*
> Autobiography

Throughout the history of the western world, the Scriptures . . . have been the greatest instigators of revolt against the worst forms of clerical and political despotism. The Bible has been the Magna Charta of the poor and of the oppressed.

> —*Thomas Henry Huxley, from*
> Controverted Questions, *1892*

Even those who do not believe that the Bible is the revelation of God, will admit that it is the supreme revelation of man.
—*William Lyon Phelps, from* Reading the Bible, *1919*

In the Old Testament stories the peace of daily life in the house, in the fields, and among the flocks, is undermined by jealousy over election and the promise of a blessing. . . . [T]he perpetually smouldering jealousy and the connection between the domestic and the spiritual, between the paternal blessing and the divine blessing, lead to daily life being permeated with the stuff of conflict, often with poison. The sublime influence of God here reaches so deeply into the everyday that the two realms of the sublime and the everyday are not only actually unseparated but basically inseparable.
—*Erich Auerbach, from* Mimesis, *1946*

All human history as described in the Bible may be summarized in one phrase, God in Search of Man.
—*Abraham Joshua Heschel, from* God in Search of Man, *1955*

To regard the Tanak [Hebrew Bible] as sacred is reasonable, but its sanctity ought to be impressed on us by study, rather than assumed beforehand. Too easily the vocabulary of religion—words like righteousness and sin—tends to become mere slogans, devoid of meaning. To call the biblical writings Sacred Scripture is to put over them a curtain which can conceal their form and meaning. Such unthinking attribution of sanctity compounds the obscurity of the Tanak. Any ancient library is hard to read and understand. Because the contents of biblical life and thought are already blurred through antiquity and distance, an unconsidered attitude [that] the writings are "sacred" can move the onlooker even beyond haziness into blindness itself.
—*Samuel Sandmel, from* The Hebrew Scriptures, *1963*

The Bible is clearly a major element in our own imaginative tradition, whatever we may think we believe about it. It insistently raises the question: Why does this huge, sprawling, tactless book sit there inscrutably in the middle of our cultural heritage . . . , frustrating all our efforts to walk around it?
—*Northrop Frye, from* The Great Code, *1982*

NOTES